Echoes of the Lost Eden

Robert Dobbs

DEDICATION

Dedicated to the courageous people of Venezuela, whose unflinching tenacity in the face of misfortune continues to motivate all of us.

And to honor the memories of those who gave their lives in the fight for a better and more liberated future, the sacrifice that you made will never be forgotten.

CONTENTS

"Fellow citizens! I blush to say this: Independence is the only benefit we have acquired, to the detriment of all the rest. All who served the revolution have ploughed the sea".

Simón Bolívar

ACKNOWLEDGMENTS

The process of writing this book has been an arduous one, and it is inconceivable that it could have been completed without the love, support, and encouragement of a large number of people. I am both awestruck and indebted to each one of them in the deepest possible way.

I would want to offer my sincere gratitude to my wife. Your everlasting faith in me, your patience over innumerable late nights, as well as your unflinching love and support, have been the pillars around which my strength has been built.

My sincere gratitude goes out to all of the scholars, historians, and journalists whose hard work gave me access to important material and insights into the complexities of Venezuela's social, political, and historical terrain. Without their efforts, I would not have been able to gain this knowledge.

I want to express my deepest gratitude to the numerous people in Venezuela who took the time to tell me about their lives, how they feel, and what they hope for the future. Your bravery and tenacity to overcome adversity are very motivating. This book is an homage to both you and the unyielding tenacity of the people in your country.

I owe an enormous amount of gratitude to my friends for their support, insightful criticism, and never-ending supply of coffee; they were essential to my productivity as a writer.

I would want to extend my gratitude to all of you, my readers, for accompanying me on this adventure. I have high hopes that this book has provided you with a glimpse into a fascinating and mind-bogglingly complicated universe.

This book is dedicated, in the last place, to all of those people who live in whatever part of the world and have hopes for a better and more liberated future. I pray that all of us will keep believing, working, and struggling for a better tomorrow.

With the deepest thanks in my heart,

INTRODUCTION

In some ways, it was the best of times, and in other ways, it was the worst of times. Venezuela, a country blessed with abundant natural beauty and a wealth of untold natural resources, is on the brink of undergoing momentous transformation. All of these things, from towering peaks to lush plains, bustling cities to sleepy villages, laughing and music floating through the air, and everything in between, were impacted by a common unease. For far too many years, the nation had been forced to exist under the shadow of an authoritarian rule. People spoke softly and in hushed tones about change as they did so in the secluded areas of cafes and in the seclusion of their own homes.

Nevertheless, even inside this atmosphere of terror, there were some people who dared to dream. Alejandro, a devoted military man, started having second thoughts about the dictatorship after having served it for such a long time. He was a man of honor who was bound by an ethical code that the dominant power in the land had long since forgotten. In another section of the country, a journalist named Sofia who was deeply committed to her work pursued with dogged determination the truth that was concealed by the smoke and mirrors of the administration. The soldier and the writer were about as different from one another as it is possible to get, yet they were brought together by a shared desire for a new Venezuela, which was their common goal and purpose.

They were all going in different directions when all of a sudden, they found themselves sucked into the vortex of revolt, and as a result, their lives were inextricably entwined. Their destiny was intertwined as they made their way through the turbulence toward freedom, and each step they took brought them one step closer to the eye of the storm.

As they traversed the intricate maze of resistance and revolution, their paths would cross and re-cross in a variety of settings, ranging from the military barracks to the newsroom, as well as the impenetrable rainforests to the busy city streets. They would encounter tests and challenges, emotional anguish and loss, but through it all, they would find strength in one another, love for one another, and hope for the future.

This is their version of the story. A tale of bravery and tenacity, illustrative of the unconquerable spirit of the human race that refuses to be subdued. This is the tale of a country on the cusp of a revolution and of a people eager to return the land that was taken from them.

We would like to welcome you to a story of defiance and redemption, a history of heroes formed in the middle of conflict and anarchy. A journey into the heart of Venezuela, where the echoes of a lost Eden inspire a daring new world. This is a journey into the heart of Venezuela.

The revolution has officially begun, and this brings the curtain up on the stage. The lights begin to go down, and as soon as everyone is still, our narrative will start. Let us accompany Alejandro and Sofia as they begin on this adventure that will change the course of their lives. We would like to welcome you to the echoes of the lost Eden, a place where the spark of revolt sparks a light of hope and transformation.

CHAPTER 1 "EDEN LOST"

Once upon a time, the pulsating center of Caracas served as the soul of Venezuela. It was a vibrant hub of life, color, and music. It had long since become a desolate wasteland, yet the spectral echoes of what it had been could still be heard there. Layers of filth and grit obscured the vivid colors of the city's street art, which was a proud representation of the city's cultural history. The unrelenting plague of poverty and hunger has reduced what were once lively marketplaces to skeleton buildings, which have had their carcasses hollowed out. The low murmur of despair and the bitter wail of the poor had taken the place of the once-constant banter and laughter that reverberated from the city walls.

Alejandro, a man who had previously served in the military, was seen walking around the empty streets. His formerly formidable physique has become noticeably less so as the burden of a nation's grief took its toll. His previously well starched uniform now sagged loosely across his frame, bearing the weight of his growing disenchantment with the world. His sunken eyes, hollowed out by the ghosts of wars fought, flashed with the remnants of an unbroken spirit, a monument to his indomitable perseverance. His eyes were hollowed out by the ghosts of battles fought.

Sofia, a journalist whose work had borne witness to Venezuela's plunge into anarchy, sat in a modest apartment across the city viewing the specter of the once-thriving Plaza Bolivar. From there, she could see the ghost of the plaza. Her formerly brilliant eyes, which previously possessed the curiosity and ardor of an enthusiastic journalist, were now burdened by the gloomy reality that she wrote about. Her fingers moved gracefully across the typewriter as she recorded the despondent symphony of the nation that she cherished.

Alejandro and Sofia, two people who came from various walks of life, were connected by the painful strands that their nation's sorrow had woven between them. Their hopes were lost in the sea of corruption, persecution, and ineptitude that had inundated their nation. Their dreams, like those of their fellow residents, were bound by the iron grasp of a repressive dictatorship.

The day was drawing to a close, but the city, which was previously famous for the spectacular sunsets it delivered, now just provided a melancholy twilight. Instead of casting a bright, golden glow over the city as it set, the sinking sun gave the appearance of bleeding into the horizon, coloring the sky with various colors of sorrow. The coming of night, rather of bringing with it a calm conclusion to the day, acted only as a spooky reminder of the repressive system that thrived in the darkness.

Nevertheless, there were still flames of hope flickering persistently, even in the midst of this crushing misery. In spite of the hardships that conflict and grief had instilled in Alejandro's heart, he continued to tenaciously believe in the resilience of his people. His intellect, which had been honed through years of military training to plan and execute battles, desired to fan the flames of disobedience that would set his people free from their shackles.

In the meanwhile, despite the challenges she was facing, Sofia's tenacity remained unshaken. She offered a voice to those who did not have one, putting light on the harsh reality of the situation with each word that she published. Her poems, which shone like a lighthouse in the middle of the engulfing gloom, offered her people a glimpse of hope and served as a gentle reminder that they were seen, heard, and not forgotten.

Alejandro and Sofia had not yet come across one another in their own fights against the crises at this point in time. But fate, which had been molded by the flames of revolt and the echoes of an Eden that had been lost, had already begun plotting a route for their approaching meeting. They had no idea that their unified front would spark a revolution, one that would pose a threat to the Maduro administration and provide Venezuela with the opportunity to recapture her lost Eden.

Alejandro made his way through the twisting alleyways of Caracas as the last embers of sunshine were eventually extinguished out by the growing night. His eyes, which had become used to the gloom, navigated the well-known routes that had been brutally scarred as a result of the crisis. A phantom assemblage of hollow-eyed faces and emaciated bodies made up the city's population, who were dispersed around the metropolis in various locations. Their slumped forms stood in sharp contrast to the proud throng that Alejandro recalled from the days before the government when they were buzzing with activity.

When he turned his head in any direction, he was confronted with the unseen anguish of his people. A mother with sunken cheeks and empty eyes distributes the remaining crumbs of stale bread to each of her skeleton children. An elderly guy, his hands twisted like ancient roots, clung to a fading photograph of a son who had been taken from him as a result of the unrest. In the absence of toys, a group of youngsters are seen playing with stones. Their once joyful laughing has been replaced with an eerie stillness.

During this time, Sofia was safely ensconced in the quiet serenity of her chamber, which served as a stronghold that protected her from the exterior upheaval. Each tap was a deliberate movement scripted by the rhythm of the truth, and her fingers danced over the keyboard like a ballerina performing a pas de deux. The lamplight played tricks on her eyes, throwing shadows that made the determination imprinted on her face appear even more stern. Every word that she wrote and every narrative that she recounted was a significant act of revolt against the oppressive silence that was enforced by the state.

Tonight, she told the story of an elderly lady named Rosa, who had worked as a botanist in the past. The once-proud display of exotic flowers and aromatic plants that was Rosa's garden has been reduced to a bare stretch of land in recent years. Rosa, who used to provide the youngsters in the neighborhood with food from the fruits that grew on her trees, was now on the verge of famine herself. As Sofia was writing, her stomach turned as she thought of Rosa's loss. But she also respected Rosa's ability to push through difficult times. The elderly lady continued to plant, despite everything that had happened, placing seeds of hope in the barren soil.

After making his way back through the deserted streets, Alejandro came to a stop in front of a wall covered in graffiti. It served as a canvas for defiance right in the middle of all the mayhem and destruction. It was a silent protest against the repression and corruption that the city was experiencing, and it bore the population's anguish and rage in a riot of hues. Because it mirrored Alejandro's internal struggle, the wall made Alejandro feel as though he had a physical connection to it. His own spirit reverberated with the same fiery hue, the same unyielding defiance that radiated from hers.

As Alejandro and Sofia traveled further into the night apart from one another due to the devastation of the city, they carried with them the germs of an uprising that was only beginning to take root. They were not yet aware that their journeys were gradually coming together; they were being led in this direction by the same magnetic pull of resistance, and the same echoes of a lost Eden that were resonating in their hearts.

Alejandro discovered the echoes of his own past in the skeletal remains of a school building that had been abandoned years earlier. His thoughts were filled with the echoes of youngsters laughing and the recollections of instructors who were passionate about their work. The eerie quiet that now ruled over the classrooms that were falling apart was a harrowing monument to the devastation caused by the government. Alejandro had a twinge of hopelessness with a hardening of his determination. Each scar on the landscape of his city, each witness of pain, served as a rallying cry for him to take up weapons.

His attention was drawn to a painting that was painted over but could still be read at the entrance to the school. "El futuro de la nación" - The future of the country, it asserted. Alejandro traced the words, with each letter serving as a reminder of what was at risk in the situation. Even though the future of their nation was being starved and suffocated by the weight of corruption and tyranny, Alejandro was not prepared to let that future perish.

In another part of the city, Sofia's chamber could be heard echoing with the percussive rhythm of her typing. She was relating the tale of a young kid named Carlos, who had to stop going to school and get a job in order to take care of his sick mother. His hopes of one day becoming a physician were shattered when they found themselves in the precarious position that they were in. His experience served as a jarring illustration of the innumerable opportunities that were squandered as a direct result of the crisis.

But, much like Alejandro, Sofia discovered inspiration among misery. In spite of the difficulties he faced, young Carlos clung to the possibility of a better future. He related his hope that one day he would be able to treat not just his mother but also all of the sick people in his town. Sofia's drive was reignited by his resiliency and his capacity to dream despite the destruction around him. She was writing not just tales of hopelessness, but also tales of defiance and perseverance in her writings. They represented her contribution to the gathering tumult of insurrection and served as weapons for her fight against the repressive state.

Alejandro and Sofia maintained their separate endeavors as the hours passed, completely oblivious to one another despite the fact that their goals were similar. In the midst of the rubble of his city, Alejandro stood guard like the watchful sentinel throughout the night. In her solitary stronghold, Sofia was the recorder and historian of the truth. They were two parts of the same whole, their souls tuned to the echoes of the Eden that had been lost, and their hearts throbbing to the rhythm of defiance.

Alejandro found himself in the position of standing in front of a homemade shelter, which was a torn construction of cardboard and sheets, as the first light of morning struggled to burst through the darkness. Inside, he could make out a family gathered together like a human tapestry, weaved together out of the strands of hopelessness and fortitude. The image was both a painful reminder of the harsh circumstances his people were now through and a powerful illustration of the unbreakable willpower they possessed. His chest tightened with a mixture of awe and desperation at the same time.

Exactly at that moment, a young girl with smudges of dirt on her cheeks and eyes that glowed with curiosity peered out of the shelter. When their eyes met, a conversation went on between them even though neither of them spokes a word. Alejandro saw remnants of the Venezuela that he once knew in her eyes; a Venezuela that was lively, thriving, and free. The girl, in her turn, perceived in his eyes a promise, a glimmer of the optimism that her people were desperately lacking. Alejandro's determination was strengthened as a result of this interaction, which was brief but significant. His people were not yet broken. Their spirit was still active, and for as long as it remained so, there was a purpose to fight and a possibility for them to recapture the Eden they had lost.

While all was going on, Sofia was giving her work the final touches it needed, and her heart was pounding with a mixture of tiredness and satisfaction. She had recorded the histories of her people, which included tales of hopelessness and disaster as well as tales of perseverance and strength. Her tales served as a living testimony to the indomitable spirit of the Venezuelan people, a spirit that defied defeat in spite of the challenges that were being presented to them at the time. She knew that her words were one of the few weapons that her people had against the dictatorship, and she accepted this task wholeheartedly. She felt an incredible obligation to be the voice of her people, and she embraced it.

Her thoughts wandered to the elderly woman Rosa and the kid Carlos who she had seen earlier. Their stories, despite the fact that they were tragic, had motivated her. In spite of the fact that they were starving, Rosa was adamant on planting crops, and Carlos never gave up on his ambition to become a physician. These two examples stood out like brilliant sparks against the bleak backdrop of the crisis. They were the very personification of the nation's everlasting spirit that was still alive and well. Sofia had the feeling that she was related to them. She clung to her conviction in the force of the truth and in the might of her pen in the same way that others clung to hope and the ability to persevere. They were her allies in battle, and the total strength of their soul shone like a lighthouse in the oppressive gloom.

Both Alejandro and Sofia maintained their own conflicts even as the first rays of dawn put a gentle glow on the deserted metropolis. Unbeknownst to them, they were on the point of converging; their paths were interwoven by the common echoes of a lost Eden, and their spirits were boosted by the approaching tide of revolt.

Alejandro found himself beside the city's formerly bustling center - Plaza Bolivar — as the morning sun painted the deteriorating cityscape in shades of melancholic gold. Now, the plaza was nothing more than a haunting phantom of its former magnificence and a mute witness to the cultural holocaust that had been perpetrated by the dictatorship. The once-lively square, which was packed with vendors, entertainers, and residents engaged in heated disputes, now sat silent and empty after its bustling days were over.

Alejandro's attention was drawn to the monument of Simon Bolivar as he made his way across the public area. The stone stare of the Libertador was still ferocious, still imbued with the determination of a man who battled for the independence of his people. After looking into the eyes of the stone, Alejandro discovered a mirror of his own spirit staring back at him. The battle they fought was the same, but their adversary was different. He felt a surge of resolve as he stood there in the shadow of the Libertador; it was like a cry to arms ringing from the past.

During this time, Sofia was gazing out her window at the first rays of sunlight of the new day. She watched as the sun began to rise beyond the horizon and sent a gentle glow over the city. She had been up all night, and although her fingers were cramped from the continual dance on her typewriter, she felt an energizing feeling of success. She had been up all night. She was well aware that the things she spoke were more than just anecdotes; rather, they were lifelines, strands of hope sewn into a fabric of resiliency.

Her gaze landed on the picture of her mother, a fearless reporter who had been Sofia's primary source of motivation when she first picked up a pen. She recalled her mother's remarks, which were, "Sofia, the truth is the first casualty in a regime like this." It is our responsibility to safeguard it and ensure that it continues to exist. We are the keepers of the truth, and we speak for those who have no other voice. Her mother's words had never seemed more pertinent, and when Sofia glanced at her reflection in the window, she saw not just a journalist but also a warrior, with her pen serving as her weapon and her words acting as her shield. Her mother's words had never seemed more pertinent.

Alejandro and Sofia found themselves in a position where they were on the verge of something really important as soon as the sun came up. They had not yet met, but their souls were already joined because they had the same unwavering resolve and the same echoes of a lost Eden that echoed inside their hearts. Although they had not yet met, they were already bonded. They were heading towards one other unwittingly as they traversed the barren metropolis; one of them was moving among the ruins, and the other was moving within the limits of her apartment. They were being attracted by the inexorable pull of destiny and revolution.

Alejandro, bolstered by the hope that a new day would bring, navigated his way through the maze-like streets of Caracas, his heart filled with a newly discovered resolve. In the light of the approaching morning, he studied the city, which was engaged in a stoic struggle against oppression that was evident in every broken wall and in every face that was empty. He went past an impromptu classroom where youngsters, whose spirits were unbroken in spite of the challenges they were facing, were gathering around a volunteer teacher. Their pure visages, which were marked with a tenacity that was eerily similar to his own, gave him the strength to keep fighting for a better tomorrow.

Back in her room, Sofia was frantically collecting her belongings while her heart raced with a mixture of nervousness and excitement about the upcoming exam. She was ready to set off on a tour into the heart of Caracas, with the objective of revealing the terrible reality of life under the government and amplifying the voices of those who were persecuted. When she glanced in the mirror, she saw a fearless journalist, the keeper of the truth, ready to fight the storm. She viewed herself as the curator of the truth.

As Sofia made her way into the heart of the city, she was immediately struck by the striking difference between the Caracas of her memory and the Caracas that stood before her. The formerly thriving metropolis, which was once a kaleidoscope of noises and colors, had become a shell of its former self, with its soul being weighed down by the harsh realities of the crisis. In spite of the hopelessness, Sofia was able to discover examples of resiliency everywhere she looked: in the face of the street seller who, despite the lack of supplies, was able to locate items to sell; in the eyes of the youngsters who, in spite of their conditions, continued to hold on to their aspirations. This was the version of Caracas that she wanted the rest of the world to see: a city that had been shattered but remained defiant in the face of oppression.

In another part of the city, Alejandro was standing in front of a wall that was covered in graffiti. This wall represented the silent resistance of his people. It said "Libertad o Muerte," which translates to "Liberty or Death." He was armed with cans of spray paint and added his own message to the collage of protest. It was a straightforward declaration, but in it were mirrored the feelings of thousands of people and their mutual hopes of attaining freedom and finding their way back to Eden.

Unknowingly, as Alejandro and Sofia explored the maze-like streets of the city, their souls became entangled by the echoes of a lost Eden and the promise of revolt. This caused them to become closer to one another as they traveled through the city. Their common goals and their common challenges were drawing them closer together, and it looked like their paths were going to cross in the middle of a city that was on the verge of upheaval.

Alejandro found himself at the entrance to a previously thriving community center that had been transformed into a food distribution site just as the morning light reached its apex and threw long, black shadows that spread across the deteriorating metropolis. A striking representation of the catastrophe that had engulfed the country was provided by the lines of individuals whose faces were drawn with the strain of their struggle as they waited in line around the block. When Alejandro saw a young mother, whose face was carved with anguish and who was pleading for an additional amount of food for her sickly kid, he felt a tightening in his chest. It was a sobering reminder of the harsh truth, a glaring illustration of why his battle was so important.

During this time, Sofia was walking around the city with her notepad and camera, recording the untold stories of the people who lived there. Each photograph that she shot was a representation of their fight, and each conversation was a penetrating look into the breadth and depth of their anguish. In the middle of the wreckage, she discovered the tale of an elderly man who had been a professor at one time but who now spent his days searching for discarded items. The desperation and the determination both shone through clearly in his eyes. Even though it was painful to hear, Sofia understood that his story had to be shared because it was important.

Alejandro's grief was turned into action when he joined the volunteers who distributed food during the middle of the day, and the sun was there to see his peaceful defiance. He gained power by helping others; each meal he served was a demonstration of his determination, and each expression of gratitude was a source of energy for his struggle. As he worked, he saw that he was surrounded not by victims but by fighters, people whose spirits remained intact in spite of the challenges they encountered.

When Sofia arrived back in the middle of the city, she found herself standing in front of a deserted bookshop with dirty windows and empty shelves. When she thought back to the days when the bookstore served as a haven for the bookworms of the city and a gathering place for intellectual discourse and debate, she felt a pang in her chest. The repressive practices of the dictatorship had claimed yet another victim, and at this moment it stood still and empty. But as she stood there, Sofia realized that the stillness in the store was perhaps a blessing in disguise. It wasn't simply a sign of tyranny; it was also a rallying cry to fight back, a compass pointing her in the direction of her mission.

Alejandro and Sofia resumed their excursions as the city sweltered under the stifling heat, making their way through the labyrinth of ruins and resistance. They had not yet met one another, and their lives had not yet collided. But their spirits were already united, and their hearts were already pounding to the rhythm of the same dream. It was a dream of a liberated Venezuela, of an Eden that had been regained.

As the day turned into the evening and a hazy twilight descended over the city, Alejandro found himself at a secret meeting at a secluded place with a group of like-minded rebels who were getting together to talk about their resistance. They discussed the situation, developed a game plan, and bolstered their determination while their faces were lighted only by the dull glimmer of a solitary lamp. Even though Alejandro was new to this, he experienced a strong feeling of belonging. These people were his allies; their aspirations were similar to his own, and their bravery stoked the fire within him.

In another part of the world, Sofia found herself in a lively marketplace where the air was filled with the heady aroma of ripe fruit and leather that had been used for a long time. In an otherwise chaotic metropolis, it seemed like a sliver of normalcy had been preserved here, but it was all an act. The stuff was few, the prices were high, and the employees' forced smiles on customers. As she made her way through the crowd, she came upon an elderly lady named Rosa whose eyes seemed to tell a story. Sofia approached her and struck up a discussion, during which she learned Rosa's story, which she described as one about overcoming adversity and possessing an unbreakable will.

An increase of adrenaline began to course through Alejandro's body as he listened to the preparations for the resistance. Their tactics were a synergy of force and deception, open warfare and covert operations, intelligence and guile. They need the assistance of every hand and the dedication of every heart, and Alejandro was prepared to provide. As he declared his loyalty to the organization, he had a sense of purpose that was greater than it had ever been before. He was no longer a lone viewer; rather, he was a participant in the uprising and a member of the group that was working to recapture its Eden.

Back in the marketplace, Sofia's discussion with Rosa was more than simply an interview; it was an enlightenment. The elderly woman, despite her difficulties, was working a little patch of ground by sowing seeds in the hope that tomorrow will be better. Her faith was driving her ahead. When Sofia looked at Rosa, she saw a mirror of her country in her. Rosa was battered but unbreakable; she had been dragged to her knees but she refused to collapse. The tale of Rosa, her unending spirit, was the city's beating heart, and Sofia was determined to make sure that everyone in the globe got to hear it.

Alejandro and Sofia resumed their crusades as the twilight shroud settled upon the city. Unaware of one another, they were united by the echoes of an Eden that had been lost. Their ways were intended to cross, and the fulfillment of their own aspirations was predetermined to coincide. But for the time being, they were nothing more than two souls making their way through a metropolis on the verge of collapse as the tempo of defiance and hope pounded in their hearts.

Alejandro found himself back at his modest house, a little flat that carried the weight of neglect, as the night's blanket of darkness enveloped him and the sky remained dark. A solitary bulb flickered in the room, generating lengthy shadows that wavered back and forth in a manner that appeared to mirror Alejandro's thoughtful demeanor. His thoughts were racing, racing over the memories of the day, the faces of his newly found allies, and the unspoken pledge he had given to the people of his city. His mind was a whirlwind.

His mind went back to the wall that was covered in graffiti and which he had noted earlier. "Libertad o Muerte," he said to himself, the words reverberating throughout the emptiness of his apartment. "Libertad o Muerte." It was more than just a catchphrase; it was a personal commitment and a pledge that he had made to both his people and to himself. He felt the weight of the choice as he painstakingly wrote it out on a sheet of paper one letter at a time. He was now an active participant in the struggle for their liberation and a member of the resistance movement.

In another part of the city, Sofia was seated in front of her typewriter. The rhythmic tapping of the keys could be heard throughout her apartment, which was otherwise silent. She was recording Rosa's history, and her fingers were racing over the keyboard as she attempted to capture the essence of the elderly woman's soul in the narrative she was writing. As she wrote, her chest hurt because every word brought back a bitter memory of the persecution that her people had to endure, and every syllable was a monument to their resiliency.

The room was illuminated with a warm glow from her desk lamp, and the buzz of her thoughts could be heard throughout the space. She was more than a journalist; she was a recorder of the human spirit, a witness to their struggle, and a participant in their uprising. She was a part of all of these things. She found herself saying "Libertad o Muerte" as she typed the final word and then took the paper out of the printer. It was a vow, an unspoken commitment that she had unintentionally made to her city and to the people who lived there.

Both Alejandro and Sofia, in their separate neighborhoods, had an unexplainable sense of connection to their hometown and the people who lived there as the night wore on. They continued to battle with the same tenacity, and their spirit never wavered. They were oblivious to the fact that they had made the same pledge into the darkness, but the reverberations of their vows could be heard across the sleepy city, weaving their destinies together. Even though they had not yet been facing to face, their spirits had already connected via the mutual echoes of a vanished Eden and a yearning for independence.

Alejandro, unable to sleep, spent the middle of the night on the roof of his building. Below him, the metropolis sprawled, its lights flitting like unsure stars over the huge metropolitan landscape. A car honked in the distance, a dog barked, and he could make out the muffled laughing of city dwellers. Strangely, he felt at peace in this isolation, the city's calm pulse matching his own.

He thought back on the young mother, the children, and his fellow rebels whom he had helped that day. Their courage and determination inspired him, and he found himself identifying with their hopes and goals. He prayed silently for their safety, their strength, and their independence as he surveyed the metropolis below. He kept saying, "Libertad o Muerte," as if it were a chant, reiterating their undying devotion to their common goal.

Sofia experienced a similar sense of isolation in a different part of the city. After finishing the day's work and transcribing Rosa's story, she went out onto her balcony and watched the city's quiet story unfold. The glow of faraway cities, the stillness of the night, and the gentle air that carried stories of fortitude all served as reminders of her mission. The day's encounters with people like Rosa and the kids and the destitute street seller all came flooding back to her thoughts. Their accounts served as motivation for her, driving her toward their goals.

She was looking at the picture of her mother, her rock and her compass. She felt a surge of determination as she stared at the picture. She was aware of the difficulty of the task ahead of her, but she felt prepared. Her words, "Libertad o Muerte," echoed through the darkness, a solemn commitment to her city and her people.

Alejandro and Sofia found comfort in their silence as night gave way to morning, the echoes of their secret promises still lingering in the air. They hadn't met yet, hadn't realized they had something in common. However, their souls were already joined together by the beat of a forgotten paradise and the hope of a fresh start.

The dawn's first rays bathed the city in a golden glow, bringing the otherwise sleepy landscape to life. After a night of reflection and isolation, Alejandro felt pulled to the city's dawn. The distant buzz of traffic, the hushed chatter of an opening market, and the pulsating music of life greeted him as he descended to the streets of Caracas.

Back to the graffiti wall, he followed the lines of the phrases he had painted the day before with his gaze. It said, "Libertad o Muerte." The wall became a canvas of defiance and a mural of their shared ambitions as the early sun illuminated the spray-painted messages. Alejandro was pleased with himself, realizing that his defiance was contributing to a greater uprising. He was no longer an outsider looking in; rather, he was a key figure in the history of his city and a fighter for its liberation.

Sofia, on the opposite side of town, was putting the last touches on her luggage before setting off for another day of digging out secrets and fighting back against the stillness. When she reached for her camera, she knew she had to act quickly. She was recording more than just stories; she was recording lifelines that allowed the oppressed to communicate with the outside world. She fought with her words and her pictures, and she was more than a journalist.

She left her apartment and strolled out into the crisp, revitalizing morning air of the city. The city had woken up and was bustling with the activity of a new day. She felt the beat of Caracas in her soul, and the might of her people in her veins. Feeling a sense of belonging, she wandered through the streets, her eyes catching the first rays of morning bouncing off the graffiti walls. As the city's struggles became her own, she became one with them. "Libertad o Muerte," she said softly, her voice blending with the beating of the city's awakening.

A new day had begun, and Alejandro and Sofia went on with their separate journeys, never expecting to meet. They had the same experience; their stories intertwined. They were two hearts tied together by the promise of revolt and the echoes of a lost Eden in the city they both called home.
As the morning progressed, Alejandro found himself in a stressful situation at the location where the food was being distributed. Due to the supply not being able to keep up with the ever-increasing demand, there was a shortage. He noticed that the line was becoming agitated as a result of the uncertainty over their future nourishment. He was well aware of the tangible tension that pervaded the throng like a live wire, and he sensed that the delicate equilibrium was about to be upset.

He spoke in a calm tone despite the ever-increasing din in an effort to appease the audience. On the other hand, his remarks were like a pebble against the flood, and the wave of discontent gobbled them up. A fight broke out, with the men's desperation turning them into barbarians. Alejandro found himself in the thick of the conflict, with his heart thumping against his chest as he attempted to bring harmony back to the situation. He was able to sense the terror, the hopelessness, the rage, and all of the raw emotions that were a direct mirror of their fight.

In another part of the city, Sofia found herself in the middle of an underground market, which was a bustling hub of activity related to the black market. The location resembled a swarm with its whispered conversations, rapid transactions, and wary looks all going on at the same time. The level of anxiety in the air was palpable, and the stakes and hazards were both quite high. A single blunder or heated voice might tilt the scales and turn the market into a battlefield.

She navigated her way through the crowd while concealing her camera and keeping her senses on high alert. She was not a member of the group, and her presence and activities were not appreciated. She was acutely aware of people's wary glances, the whispered conversations, and the sense of impending danger. But she continued to fight, her will unyielding and her focus unmistakable. She was here to find the truth, to reveal the uglier side of their suffering, and she was not going to back down from this fight.

The anxiety never let up during the course of the day. It hung in the air like a thick cloud, producing lengthy shadows that were rather black. After successfully regaining control of the situation, Alejandro discovered that he was exhausted, the events of the day serving as a vivid reminder of the hopeless truth. However, this just served to strengthen his resolve, and he refused to let his spirit buckle under the pressure of their conflict.

After sneaking around and taking a few photos, Sofia hurried out of the market, her heart thumping furiously in her chest. The day served as a reminder of their bleak situation and provided a glimpse into the most difficult aspects of their struggle. But it also strengthened her resolve, and in her heart, she could hear the words "Libertad o Muerte," which had become the motto by which she lived her life.

Alejandro and Sofia successfully maneuvered their way through the tense metropolis as the sun began to set, turning the sky various shades of orange and scarlet. Their spirits were shaken, yet they remained steadfast in their determination. Their hearts were heavy. Their journeys had not yet collided, but their tribulations were already connected. They were linked by the echoes of a lost Eden and a common vow of defiance against authority.

The city of Caracas was cloaked in a red and gold robe as the sun sank, creating an artistic caricature of their reality with hues that were too bright and too cheerful. Alejandro's body hurt, and his soul was stressed out as a result of the day's events, which weighed heavy on his shoulders. But he did not waiver in his determination. The desperation and anxiety that he had been experiencing, if anything, had only served to reinforce his devotion.

The graffiti wall came into view as he proceeded along the path leading to his flat. Its bold colors were now illuminated by the glow of the lowering sun, and the words "Libertad o Muerte" were looking back at him. In spite of all that had happened that day, the sight made him grin from ear to ear. It was their reality shown in bright hues; rebellious, unbreakable, and resilient were some of the words that sprang to mind. It was their collective aspiration shown for everyone to see, a subversive act that still carried significant weight. While he was there, Alejandro reiterated his commitment to the cause. He was going to battle for freedom, because he believed that it was worth the effort and worth the cost.

In the meantime, Sofia was making her way back home through the winding streets of Caracas, which are like a maze, while her heart was thumping in time with the pulse of the city. The fraught atmosphere of the illicit market, with its desperation-driven bargaining and subtle threats, served as a sobering reminder of the precarious situation they were in. However, it was also a demonstration of their tenacity and will. They had made it through the storm and were clinging to the tiniest shreds of hope that they could find.

After she returned home, she processed the images that she had been able to take. Her heart broke as the pictures began to come to life because of the hopelessness that they portrayed. However, despite the suffering, there was a remarkable capacity for recovery. The images served as evidence of both their perseverance and their difficulty. It served as a reminder of why she was putting her life in danger and why the words and pictures she shared were important. She served as the voice of her people, and the fight they were engaged in became her mission. She sat down at her typewriter with the photographs in her hand, and she started recounting the events of the day. It was more than just a narrative; it was their life, and the struggle that they were engaged in. As she wrote the final character, she repeated the oath that she had taken earlier: "Libertad o Muerte."

Caracas, the capital of Venezuela, fell into a restless slumber as soon as night struck. However, Alejandro and Sofia still had a significant amount of work to complete for the day. They were, in their own ways, recording the fight that was taking on in their city; their acts were a revolt against the repression, and their lives were a tribute to the resiliency of the people. They were, unbeknownst to one another, interweaving their stories into the very fabric of the city, their single vows of "Libertad o Muerte" reverberating throughout the stillness of the night.

Their souls were entwined as they lived under the same sky in Caracas, and their determination did not waver. Alejandro and Sofia, two lone warriors in the middle of a bleeding metropolis, had just started out on their adventure. Their stories had not yet intersected, and their fates had not yet come into conflict with one another. Their city, their Eden, may have been destroyed at this point, but the hope that they shared for Libertad was not yet dead. The battle has barely started between them.

CHAPTER 2 "ECHOES OF THE PAST"

In the peace and seclusion of his chamber, Alejandro realized that he was rummaging through the maze of his past recollections. The room, with its peeling wallpaper and worn-out furnishings, held memories of a period that had long since passed, a time when laughing could be heard filling the halls and dreams were emblazoned on the walls. This chamber served as a time capsule, protecting his heritage and his origins.

The memories of Alejandro's boyhood came flooding back to him with such vividness that it was as if he was watching a movie in his head. He recalled a period when Caracas was a city of dreams, with a spirit that was dynamic and a future that looked optimistic. He was the youngest of three children and the only one of his family to be born into a household that was of middle class. His family was one that believed in the enchantment of dreams and the strength of knowledge.

His father was a guy of brilliance and strong moral convictions, and he taught at the Central University of Venezuela. He recalled how his father's eyes would light up with excitement whenever he spoke history, the events of the past coming to life via his father's vivid narrations. His mother was a nurse, and she was a courageous and kind person. Her recounting of the happy, painful, and hopeful moments that occurred during her shifts at the medical center was fascinating.

They enjoyed an uncomplicated life, but it was one that was rich with love and hopes for both of them. Alejandro recalled the numerous days he spent playing football in the tight alleyways of their neighborhood, the evenings that were filled with his father's history lectures, and the nights that were calmed by his mother's lullabies. Those were the days of childhood, the days of serenity and innocence.

Nevertheless, as Alejandro reflected on these recollections, he couldn't help but experience a sharp pang of discomfort. Because Caracas as he remembered it from his boyhood no longer existed, and in its stead was a city that was fighting for its life. The lessons of history that his father had taught him were now a part of his own experiences; the past and the present were blending into one excruciating reality for him. His mother's lullabies had been replaced by the symphony of turmoil, and the struggle of the city had become their collective nightmare.

When Alejandro saw the faded photo of his family laying on the table, he plunged even more into the shadowy parts of his past. In his mind, he had left the confines of his room and been transported to their former home, a modest but welcoming place full of warmth, laughter, and hope. His mind was flooded with memories from a day that had started off like any other but had left an indelible mark on his young heart.

All around the country, people were on strike to protest the government's increasing authoritarianism. Principled as he was, his father had decided to join the protest because he thought it was his duty to the community. When Alejandro was just thirteen, he didn't really grasp the gravity of the situation. Nonetheless, he remembers the tight atmosphere, his father's determined attitude, and his mother's worry lines that were becoming increasingly apparent.

There was a harsh crackdown on the protestors, and word of it spread as dusk approached. Alejandro remembered the panic that had gripped the situation and how the wait for his father's return had grown more agonizing by the second. Alejandro fully understood the cost of their fight for independence when he watched his father come through the door injured and shattered but unbowed. The day he was forced to face the harsh truths of their culture was the day his childhood ended and he was thrust into the adult world.

The political crisis worsened, the economic stability they had counted on collapsed, and the city of dreams began its descent into a city of despair in the years that followed. His family relied only on his mother's salary, and the streets where he formerly played football were transformed into sites of demonstrations and police barricades. After his father was sacked from the university for political reasons, his mother's job became the sole source of money for their family.

His parents may have had a tough go of it, but they never gave up.
So that his son's education wouldn't suffer as a result of their
circumstances, his father kept teaching him, turning their living room
into a makeshift classroom. His mother was more dedicated than
ever, working extra shifts to provide for her family. And young but
resolute Alejandro promised to fight for the Caracas he knew, vowing
to restore it to its former splendor.

On the other side of town, Sofia was looking over her old
journals, which she had filled with detailed accounts of her life up to
that point. Both of her parents were reporters, and she inherited their
penchant for storytelling and appreciation of language. She spent her
childhood as a reclusive observer, taking in whatever, she could with
her keen eyes and letting her imagination do the rest.

Sofia's parents were her first educators, demonstrating her the
value of language and exposing her to the world of narrative. They
had faith in the press's ability to get to the truth and in the
importance of free speech. She grew up hearing their tales and
gaining insight into the world from their perspectives.

Her dad was an editor at a major newspaper and was well-known
for his investigative reporting. He was an honest man who never
shied away from seeking the truth. Sofia recalled how he frequently
worked until the wee hours of the night; his face lit by the desk lamp
as his fingers danced across the keyboard.

Her mother was a photojournalist who managed to capture the
essence of their hometown in her photographs. Her photographs
were a visual story of their era, revealing her meticulous attention to
detail. When Sofia was younger, her mother would take her on
picture walks around the city and show her how to observe things
from a photographer's perspective.

The corridors resounded with the spirited conversations of
writers, musicians, and thinkers who frequented their home. Sofia
listened in silence, taking in all of their talk, their enthusiasm, and
their commitment. She became passionate in journalism, storytelling,

and investigating the truth as a result of these conversations.

But as Sofia read over her diary entries, she was brought back to the day that altered the course of their lives. The essay her dad had written exposing government corruption had just been published that day. Their phone was ringing off the line, and their home was surrounded by reporters after the publication of the piece. However, everything changed that night when her father was kidnapped and their home was robbed.

Her mom had comforted her, and the two of them had cried together. Nonetheless, Sofia recalled her mother's remarks, which she had heard despite the commotion. Truth is strong, and it will win out in the end. Never give up sharing your experience.

Sofia watched her mother go from photojournalist to activist in the years that followed, using her camera as a weapon in the fight against oppression. And so, like her parents before her, Sofia turned to the arts of writing and photography as her means of self-expression and defiance.

After that day, the previously lively house was filled with a profound hush. The once-joyous talks were replaced by whispered conversations, and the once-frequent visits from journalists were replaced by suspicious looks from neighbors. They were under constant surveillance by the tyrannical eye of the government, with every action and word being scrutinized and evaluated.

In spite of everything, Sofia and her mother continued on. Her mother was a well-known photojournalist in the past, but she now worked for a clandestine publication, and her pictures captured the grim reality of the conflict. And Sofia, who was developing into a budding journalist in her own way, recounted their daily trials in her writings, with her words giving a vivid picture of the terrible surroundings.

Sofia recalled her first experience dealing with the underground economy, which was an inescapable aspect of their new world. She had just turned sixteen at the time, and her mother was ill; both of them required medications that could not be found at the neighborhood pharmacies. Her hands were shaking and her pulse was hammering as she made her first purchase of illegal medicine in the back alleyways of Caracas. There, in the middle of whispered murmurs and veiled threats, she made the purchase. It was on that day that she really comprehended the seriousness of their predicament and the scope of the deterioration of their city.

Even as the situation became more dire, Sofia and her mother clung to each other for support. Their similar experiences of loss bound them together, and their commitment to a common goal fueled their tenacity. They worked together, their words and pictures constituting a covert uprising against those who oppressed them and their struggles forming the basis of a common narrative. The experiences that they shared with Sofia began to fill up her diaries, and her writings became a tribute to their resiliency.

Sofia would seek consolation in her recollections on the days when she felt like she was about to be overcome by hopelessness. She recalled that before to the crisis, Venezuela was a country that was abundant in culture and wealth, and its people were friendly and hospitable. She recalled Caracas in all of its splendor, the city's essence enduring over the ages and its heartbeat remaining strong. She recalled the cheerful festivities, the colorful festivals, the busy marketplaces, and the buzzing cafés.

Sofia was overcome with an overwhelming sensation of melancholy as she wrote down her recollections. The Venezuela of her recollections stood in sharp contrast to the country as it was at the present time. But even despite all of the mayhem, Sofia maintained her optimism. She saw it in the unyielding tenacity of her mother, in the unyielding resistance of the people, and in the graffiti art that graced the walls of their city. And with every letter she typed, every picture she took, she made a solemn promise to maintain that sense of optimism.

In the center of the city, which was now more of a haunted village than a bustling metropolis, Sofia discovered her mission, and the ruins of the city only served to reinforce her resolve. She maneuvered through the winding passageways of their shack town with her camera draped over her neck and her diary never far from her side. Her comprehension of their suffering was deepened with each new face she saw and each new tale she listened to, which fueled her desire to get to the bottom of things and reveal the truth.

Her writing became more daring, and her photographs, which captured the brutal truth of their situation, became more arresting. Long lines of people waiting outside of grocery shops without basic essentials, youngsters searching through rubbish for bits of food, and hospitals short crucial medicines were all things that her pen and her lens captured.

She was able to recall a specific event that stuck out in her mind. It was a woman she had met in one of the makeshift clinics; her face was a map of the hardships she had through and the strength she had found. She had previously worked as a teacher, but now days she spends her time searching for food and medicine so she can treat her sick kid. Her account was a gloomy reminder of the way in which their lives had been irrevocably changed, and of the way in which a formerly prosperous middle class was now on the verge of utter poverty.

Nevertheless, the spirit of the woman was what struck Sofia the most. Despite the hopelessness she felt, she had not given up. Her comments reflected the tenacity and resolve of the Venezuelan people, as she delivered them with a fiery sense of purpose. She spoke firmly and her eyes did not waver as she looked straight ahead. "We are a nation of survivors," she remarked. "We might be beaten, but we're not broken."

These were the words that Sofia kept in her head throughout their ordeal, and they served as a lighthouse for her as she navigated the treacherous back alleyways. It was a fight that they had all been through together; their histories were intertwined into the fabric of their city, and their resiliency was the legacy they left behind together.

On the other side of town, Alejandro also discovered that he was preoccupied with thoughts of the past. The living room had been converted into a school, football games had been played in small passageways, and animated conversations had taken place at the dinner table; echoes of the past were all about him. Despite this, he was not overcome with hopelessness. Instead, he uncovered a strong feeling of drive within himself.

This simple room, which had served as a safe haven for him in the past, was now his battleground. Alejandro was nudged in the direction of the route that his father had previously traveled by the reverberation of his father's voice, his teachings, and his tales, all of which were contained within these walls. He was aware that it was his responsibility to take up the mantle and fight against the corruption and tyranny that had taken hold of their nation, but the issue of how he was going to do this continued to torment him.

When Alejandro would wake up in the morning, he would be greeted by a cacophony of whispered murmurs and apprehensive sighs. As he made his way through the once-bustling streets of Caracas, he was greeted by vacant looks and phony grins from the people he saw. A terrible sense of hopelessness had taken its place in lieu of the vibrant life that had once flourished in this location.

Despite this, there was an indomitable spirit among the people that could not be destroyed. In spite of the difficulties, they got out of bed every morning with the expectation that things will get better tomorrow. They worked hard and struggled for their own existence, their will remaining unshaken. And it was precisely this energy that Alejandro hoped to reawaken so that it might be channeled into a collective power that they could use to fight their oppressors.

Alejandro thought back on his pals, their shared ambitions, and their common sense of defiance. They had spent their childhoods together, forging their bond on the schoolyard playgrounds and strengthening it in the classrooms. However, the crisis had dispersed them, and their formerly shared dreams had become a thing of the past.

Carlos, another one of his close pals, had decided to take up arms and fight violently against the government and had joined the ranks of the armed rebels. Alejandro recalled the day Carlos had gone, his eyes burning with rage and his voice crackling with a resolute resolve as he spoke about the event. Alejandro was unable to reconcile his beliefs with Carlos's techniques, despite the fact that Carlos supported their purpose. Alejandro believed in their cause.

As Alejandro worked his way through the events of his past and the reality of his present, he found himself in a position where he needed to make a decision. A choice that would define the path that his life would take, between taking part in an armed uprising or participating in a nonviolent demonstration. Despite the fact that it was an impossible load to carry, he was forced to make a decision about it.

Alejandro, in spite of the conflict going on inside of him, discovered that he was drawn to the protests that were nonviolent. He heard the lessons his father had taught him echoed in their words, and their nonviolent opposition was a demonstration of the power of the human spirit. He recalled the words that his father had spoken to him growing up, "In violence, we lose our humanity." We discover our fortitude through the practice of nonviolent opposition." These comments continued to reverberate in his head as he made the initial step toward following in his father's footsteps and becoming an activist. His father's lessons were directing him along this road.

Alejandro saw himself becoming increasingly active in the demonstrations as the days went into weeks. He went to meetings, participated in the organization of protests, and even led shouts out into the streets, with his voice resonating across the city as he did so. His dedication was unflinching, his determination was unshakeable, and his spirit was unshakeable. Despite this, he was unable to rid himself of the worry, the uncertainty, and the impending threat that followed their every action.

When he was walking back to his home one evening after attending a demonstration, he was confronted by a gang of guys. Despite the fact that they were disguised in civilian clothes, it was clear from their hostile glare and the threatening manner in which they carried themselves that they were government agents. They implied that his participation in the demonstrations would have terrible repercussions for him by threatening him in words but without directly confronting him. Alejandro, though, did not back down from his position, hiding his anxiety behind an air of firmness and resolution.

While he was lying in bed that night, the echoes of the past seemed to be becoming louder, and their resonance seemed to be getting stronger. He recalled the bravery of his father, how he had resisted the oppression of the government in a nonviolent manner, and how dedicated he was to their cause. And he was certain that, despite the terror and the threats, he would not back down from his position. He would keep fighting, protesting, and resisting in every way he could.

However, the worry continued to exist, and this time it was not for him but for his family. His mother and his younger sister provided him with both the support and the motivation he needed. He was unable to face the notion of putting them in danger or jeopardizing their safety in any manner as a result of his actions. But despite the fact that he was struggling with this terror, he was aware that he could not retreat and could not cave in. Their resistance and their struggle would determine their future and whether or not they would live.

As Alejandro reflected on the decision he had made, he came to the conclusion that he was fighting not just against their oppressors but also against the anxiety, uncertainty, and indifference that had crept into their lives as a result of the route they had chosen. He had taken the responsibility upon himself and made the decision to continue the heritage of his father's nonviolent fight against the oppression. It was a route that was riddled with perils and uncertainties, but it was a one that he had chosen, and it was a path that he was determined to walk down.

Alejandro began to look at the place he called home from a new angle. The collapsing buildings, the abandoned streets, and the low murmur in the air were constant reminders of the hardships they were going through and the struggle they were having against their oppressors. But even in the midst of the destruction and hopelessness, Alejandro found a glimmer of optimism and a tenacity that is inherent in the Venezuelan people.

He discovered a reflection of that tenacity in his mother. Her tenacity, unyielding commitment, and unwavering belief in the importance of her mission were an inexhaustible source of motivation for him. Despite all the challenges, she managed to keep the family together by providing them with love as a soothing remedy and her spirit as a guiding light.

More than that, his sister Mary was a bright spot in the darkness. Her childlike innocence, unwavering optimism, and ability to delight in even the smallest things were like a breath of fresh air in the dreary lives they led. Despite the challenges she faced, she was able to put a smile on her face, and her laughter echoed through her small apartment, bringing with it a sense of normalcy and a touch of former existence.

Alejandro participated more and more in the demonstrations, dedicating every moment of his waking life to the cause, and he realized that he was getting closer to his family because their struggle was bringing them all together. They spent their evenings huddled together in their living room, with the radio as their only source of information, and their shared silence was a tribute to their shared terror and hope.

One evening they were sitting together listening to the illegal radio broadcasts when suddenly a loud knock sounded at the door. This broke the silence they had shared until then. Alejandro felt his heart pounding, and his mind raced at a million miles an hour. The knocking echoed through the deserted streets, creating an ominous atmosphere accompanied by a wave of fear. When Alejandro opened the door, he was greeted by a face he had seen before, a sight that immediately took him back to his past, to his youth. It was Carlos who had done it.

Carlos, his childhood friend and partner in the rebellion, stood at his door with an exhausted face and a worried look. The boy Carlos

Alejandro remembered, always full of life and always up for an adventure, was very different from this man. He was a stark contrast. Adversity had taken its toll and instead of his usual laughter, he had a tired spirit and a grim determination.

As Carlos entered their little dwelling, his eyes quickly scanned the space, taking in the recent transformations as well as the stark reality of their life. Alejandro was able to read the worry, sorrow, and nostalgia in his eyes. He was pining for the days gone by. They sat down, the quiet between them serving as a reminder of the past they shared as well as the suffering they endured together.

"Things have changed, haven't they?" is a rhetorical question. Carlos's voice was raspy as he eventually broke the stillness, and his eyes were fixated on Alejandro the entire time. Alejandro could only nod, feeling a weight in his chest and a dryness in his throat. They were no longer the same people; their lives had taken a turn that none of them could have foreseen, and the fantasies they had shared had been replaced by a harsh reality.

After then, Carlos continued to explain about his experiences in the resistance, including the brutal battles they fought and the terrible reality of their struggle. He spoke about the lives that had been lost, the sacrifices that had been made, and the never-ending battle against those who oppressed them. His words were weighed down with sorrow, and his eyes was fixed on something in the distance.

While he listened, Alejandro's heart broke for his buddy and the way he had chosen to live his life. His non-violent demonstrations were in sharp contrast to Carlos's aggressive uprising, and as a result, he felt a wave of powerlessness sweep over him. Despite this, he was unable to shake the conviction, the belief in their cause, or the will to fight for their rights and freedom.

As Carlos recounted his experiences, Alejandro gained a new perspective on the predicament and became aware of the savagery of their fight as well as the violence that had permeated their everyday lives. He came to the conclusion that the struggle they were engaged in was not only directed against their oppressors, but also against the hopelessness, indifference, and dread that had seized control of their life.

When Alejandro went to bed that night, he couldn't help but mull over Carlos's remarks and the things he had been through in his life. He discovered that he was having second thoughts about his decisions, particularly his decision to oppose the oppression peacefully. He struggled mightily with his fears, his uncertainties, and his doubts. However, in the middle of the chaos, he discovered a sense of clarity as well as a feeling of purpose. He was well aware that he had to keep up his battle and lead his people in continuing their nonviolent resistance to their oppressors.

The words that Sofia had written, the images that she had taken, and her unwavering determination to reveal the truth all provided Alejandro with inspiration. He drew courage from his mother's unyielding faith and his sister's naive hope in the best possible outcome. He found fortitude in the tenacity of his people, in the fact that they struggled together and hoped for the same things.

Alejandro discovered his purpose and reinforced his resolve as he navigated through the echoes of his past and the reality of his present. Despite the chaos, he was able to find his mission. He was prepared to confront the difficulties that lay ahead, prepared to carry on the heritage left by his father, and prepared to fight for their freedom.

Alejandro and Sofia's participation in their nonviolent resistance became deeper as each passing day transformed into the next week. They devoted each and every waking moment to their movement, participating in meetings and helping to organize demonstrations. Their deeds did not go unpunished, as evidenced by the fact that the government is now aware of them and keeps close tabs on their operations. They did not let this dissuade them, and their determination did not waiver.

Alejandro found himself in the position of being the voice of their resistance, with his comments resonating across the city and motivating others to join their cause. He published essays and delivered lectures, with each of his words serving as a tribute to their fight for independence and their struggle. His comments were not only his own; rather, they were the voice of his people, speaking for their aspirations, anxieties, and desires.

On the other hand, Sofia decided to share their narrative via the use of her photography. The images that she took captured the harsh realities of their existence as well as the brutalities of their battle. Her shots were more than simply pictures; they were a demonstration of their struggle, their fortitude, and their optimism. They were able to capture the anguish that was written all over their features, the hopelessness that was in their eyes, and the courage that was in their determination.

The government's response was violent, despite the protesters' attempts to keep things calm. They were harassed, their families were singled out, and their houses were searched. They witnessed the taking of their companions, the silencing of their voices, and the breaking of their spirits. Despite this, they did not give in; the challenge only served to strengthen their determination.

Alejandro was pulled up by government authorities one day as he was heading back to his home after participating in a demonstration. He was crammed into a van despite his pleading, but no one paid attention to him. His worst fears were realized. He was whisked away to an undisclosed place, his loved ones having no idea where he was and fearing for his well-being as a result.

Alejandro discovered that he was the only one in the filthy cage, and his anxieties were the only company he had. He was interrogated, every word he said was analyzed, and every move he took was called into question. But Alejandro did not budge from his position; his will and his passion remained unshaken. He steadfastly remained faithful to his people and the cause he stood for, and he thus refused to reveal any information.

Alejandro's stoicism did not waver as the hours changed into days and the weeks evolved into months. He maintained his optimism, his conviction in their just cause, and his confidence in the people of his community. He was aware that they were out there, struggling for their independence, their voices being heard across the city, and their determination remaining unshaken.

In the meantime, Sofia found herself taking the lion's share of responsibility for their cause, as her part became more important than ever before. She continued to document their fight, her images serving as a jarring reminder of their suffering and her words serving as an echo of their will. She was the driving force behind the demonstrations, and her voice has become a symbol of hope and an encouragement to everyone.

Sofia's resilience increased as a direct result of Alejandro's absence. Her firmness of purpose and her doggedness in pursuing her goals became her armor, and her camera became her weapon. Her artwork served as a record of their fight, and the images she took became a guiding light in the middle of the chaos of the conflict. She was no longer only a photographer; rather, she had evolved into a storyteller, with her camera acting as the narrator to convey the account of their battle, their resistance, and their unyielding spirit.

She made advantage of her position to bring attention to the case of Alejandro's disappearance, which resulted in his face being displayed on walls all over the city and his name being whispered among the masses. The question "Where is Alejandro?" became into a rallying cry, a symbol of their combined struggle as well as their combined sense of loss.

Sofia was able to find pals in the unlikeliest of places. Maria, sister of Alejandro, joined her cause, her young energy and her passion reflecting Sofia's determination to fight for what she believed in. Their acts shook the fundamental foundations of the system, and their voices reverberated throughout the city. Together, they were a tremendous force.

Maria and Sofia experienced a loss together, which brought them closer together. They became close because of the love they had for Alejandro, and their experiences of suffering provided a tacit understanding between them. They comforted and supported one another through their experiences of loss, which served as a unifying force amongst them.

While incarcerated, Alejandro clung to the memories he had of his family and of Sofia. Every morning, before opening his eyes, he would close them and picture Sofia behind her camera, her eyes gleaming with purpose and her spirit unshaken by obstacles. He clung to the memories of his sister, whose joyous personality shone like a beacon of hope and whose laughter could be heard throughout his childhood home. He thought about his mother, her calm determination, and her unyielding confidence in the cause they were fighting for.

The time that Alejandro spent locked up was a true test of his willpower and his soul. However, every morning when he got up, he had a renewed feeling of purpose and a renewed belief in the importance of their mission. He clung to the idea that he would one day see Sofia, that he would once again hear his sister laugh, and that he would once more feel the soothing presence of his mother.

The tension in the city increased as Alejandro remained held captive for a longer period of time. The level of activity and frequency of protests increased. Sofia and Maria were at the forefront of the situation, with their voices raised and their acts becoming more daring. Their message was very clear: they would not allow themselves to be bullied or silenced in any way. Their determination was unshakeable, and their spirit remained unbroken.

In spite of the severe repression carried out by the government, the demonstrations continued to spread. As more and more individuals joined Sofia and Maria, their shared pain and their shared loss became a force that brought them closer together. They came from a variety of backgrounds, such as students, teachers, laborers, and merchants; the fact that they came from such different walks of life is a monument to their common fight and resistance.

The images taken by Sofia began to be seen much beyond the confines of their city and eventually made their way into the global community. The fight they were putting up in the globe was now becoming noticed by the outside world. The photographs that Sofia took were no longer merely pictures; rather, they had evolved into symbols that represented their struggle and served as evidence of their bravery and resiliency.

When Sofia was on her way home after a demonstration one day, she found herself surrounded by a gang of operatives from the government. They made an attempt to steal her camera, and it was evident that their goal was to stifle her voice and conceal the truth. But Sofia battled back, her determination unwavering and her spirit unshaken by the challenge. She was able to flee the scene with both her camera and her composure unharmed.

The close call that Sofia had with peril only served to strengthen her determination. She continued to keep a record of their fight, and the images she took were a source of inspiration and a representation of their defiance. Her images captured the tenacity, stubborn energy, and unwavering determination that her subjects had.

While everything was going on, Alejandro was reminiscing about his life before everything went to hell in the cell that he was currently occupying. He recalled the things that his father had said, the lessons he had taught, and the advice he had given. He recalled his father's unyielding commitment to their cause and his unrelenting efforts to secure their independence. Alejandro clung to the lessons that he had learned from his father, allowing his memories of him to serve as a source of both strength and solace through the difficult times.

Alejandro discovered peace in the reverberations of his past, his recollections serving as a demonstration of his determination and his passion. He drew courage from his father's words, the lessons he had taught him, and the insight he had shared. He discovered a source of hope in the memories of Sofia, especially her unyielding faith and her tenacious battle for their liberation.

Alejandro maintained his optimism and his trust in the resilience of his people as the passing days evolved into weeks. He had faith in their ability to persevere, their passion, and their unwavering determination. He was aware that they were out there, struggling for their independence, their voices being heard across the city, and their determination remaining unshaken.

Alejandro and Sofia clung to the memories and dreams that they had in common with one another even as the echoes of their history resonated through the present. They were able to find comfort in their recollections, which served as a monument to their tenacity and their unyielding spirit. Despite the disorder that was all around them, their confidence in one another and belief in the justness of their cause remained unshaken, and they did not allow it to dampen their spirit.

Back in the city, the spirit of resistance flourished, fueled by the people's unfaltering determination and their stubborn spirit. The images taken by Sofia continued to make the rounds, their harsh realism serving as a rallying cry for many. Her camera managed to show the resiliency of their people as well as their dogged pursuit of independence. Her photos were more than simply snapshots; they had evolved into potent emblems of the resistance movement and the quest for independence.

Their fight for freedom and their quest for justice continued unabated despite the fact that the echoes of Alejandro's speech resonated throughout the city and that Sofia's images were being passed around among the throng. They continued to resist despite the savage crackdown and the persistent tyranny, their voices soaring above the pandemonium and their energy resonating across the city.

Alejandro and Sofia were more than simply two individuals swept up in the turmoil of a revolution when it was all said and done. They were the personification of the resiliency, spirit, and unwavering determination that their people had. Their narratives, their ordeals, and the fight they put up were reverberations from their history, a demonstration of their character, and a glimmer of hope for their future.

They forged a route towards a future that is unclear but optimistic by leaving a legacy of resiliency and resistance that reverberates through the chaotic streets of Venezuela.

CHAPTER 3 "DAWN OF DESPAIR"

As the sun rose in the east, it cast long shadows over the city, foreshadowing the difficult conditions that had befallen it. The once bustling markets, teeming with people and bursting with color and bustle, were now completely deserted. The voices of merchants, the laughter of children and the hum of daily life have been replaced by an unsettling and oppressive silence. This silence has come over the neighborhood, displacing the sounds that once existed. The people of Venezuela were forced to starve constantly, and the torment this condition brought was even worse than the sweltering heat.

Sofia persevered despite the overwhelming pessimism that permeated her surroundings. She felt as if a huge rock had been pressed into her chest as she roamed the desolate streets with her camera around her neck and a memory card full of haunting images of desolation and decay. She had this experience while wearing her camera around her neck. In her images, she was able to capture the expressionless faces of children and young people, the skeletal appearance of the elderly, and the emptiness that had replaced the liveliness of her hometown.

Her images were no longer just a means of resistance, but rather a cry for help and an invitation to the rest of the world to see the horror that had come upon their country through the actions of the regime. Each click of the shutter pained her chest, for each photograph was a testament to the misery of an entire nation and the people who lived within it.

Alejandro, on the other hand, was locked in a filthy prison cell and could only watch the crisis outside his window. He was unable to do anything about it. The muffled murmurs of the security guards, the increasing frequency of the riots, and the silence that had replaced the otherwise lively sounds of the city presented a picture more frightening than any of Sofia's paintings.

The news that his mother had passed away was brought to him by one of the compassionate security guards. When he heard the news, he was completely distraught. The news took the wind out of his sails, robbed him of his vitality and made him give up all hope. It seemed as if someone had punched him in the stomach. Because he was locked in the freezing cold cell, he couldn't even mourn the loss of his mother, who had died of starvation. She had died as a result of malnutrition.

The death of Alejandro's mother was like a cruel cyclone that ripped through Sofia. She had always admired the older woman for her strength, dignity, and unwavering belief in a brighter future. Alejandro's mother was the family's rock through thick and thin, her unwavering optimism illuminating the darkest of moments. The news of her death was more than just a personal tragedy; it was a blow to their team morale and a sobering reminder of the unforgiving world in which they now found themselves.

During the wake, everyone was silent except for the muffled screams of Maria and Sofia and the occasional sniffs. The people, already weakened by hunger and sorrow, seemed to dwindle even further in number that day. They huddled together, their bodies warming one another and their shared pain providing solace.

Sofia used her camera to record the palpable air of quiet despair that hung over them. Her camera's shutter matched their muffled sobs, immortalizing their anguish, grief, and loss. Every still shot showed their pain, their fight, and their determination to persevere.

Alejandro cried himself to sleep in his cell at his tragic loss. The cold, damp walls of his cage were his only companions throughout his lonely, depressed moments. A cruel reminder of the toll their resistance and pursuit of freedom took came in the form of the news of his mother's death. The pain was searing and searingly agonizing, tearing at him like a blazing inferno.

Despite feeling completely hopeless, Alejandro found strength in his mother's memory. He thought back on how her cheerful demeanor and steady faith in the significance of their mission had calmed him. He thought back on her resilience, determination, and determination. These memories were all he had to hold on to when he was at his lowest moment in life.

While Sofia and Maria mourned in the city and Alejandro mourned in his cell, the situation deteriorated. The severity of hunger, the violence of the protests, and the brutality of the administration all rose as time went on. The once-proud and progressive metropolis is now a terrifying picture of decay and devastation.

Around the city, the iron fist of the dictatorship strengthened its hold, making the state's raw force and heartless cruelty an ever-present danger. They walked the streets with guns slung across their chests, their eyes as icy and unforgiving as the steel they carried in their hands. They quelled any whiff of discontent by stamping on it, their brutality reverberating through the deserted streets as a gruesome demonstration of their iron grip on power.

People went missing in the middle of the night, and their disappearance served as a terrifying reminder of the price that must be paid for resistance. Their screams for justice were drowned out by the unrelenting cruelty of the dictatorship, which resulted in the dissolution of families. The fear of repression was real; it was like a noose that was tightening around the city's neck and squeezing the life out of it.

with the middle of this worsening catastrophe, Sofia persisted with her objective, using her camera as her weapon against those who oppressed them. She was able to depict the terrible crackdowns, the hopelessness that was engraved into the faces of her people, and the spirit of resistance that flared persistently amidst the gloom. Each snapshot was a jolt to the stomach, a glaring reminder of the harsh reality they were living in, and a demonstration of their unbreakable will.

Sofia continued to make her way across the city despite the risks, her pulse thumping in her chest as she kept her attention fixed on the task at hand. She walked about as if she were a ghost, with quiet movements and a presence that was hardly perceptible. She kept a record of the crimes that were committed, using her camera to record the brutal reality as her soul echoed the defiance of her people.

Once Alejandro was back in his cell, his hopelessness only grew. The utter lack of sound was deafening, and the lonesomeness was intolerable. The information about the worsening catastrophe reached him in pieces; each of them was a blow to his spirit and a weight that crushed his spirit to its core.

The walls of the jail seemed to creep closer together, and there appeared to be less and less air within. Alejandro was unable to shake the visions of hopelessness that were portrayed by the pieces of information they provided. His mind was a quagmire of horrific possibilities, and the cries that resonated through the hallways of the jail became the music of his loneliness.

The memories of the people he'd left behind kept him awake at night and prevented him from getting any rest. He witnessed his mother's grin change into a shadow, felt Sofia's touch transform into a wisp of smoke, and heard Maria's laughing transform into gut-wrenching cries. The solitary confinement he was subjected to in his cell was more torturous than any form of physical abuse; it ate away at his spirit like a ruthless predator.

Alejandro refused to let go of the memories he had of his mother, despite the hopelessness that was threatening to swallow him. Her unyielding optimism and unflappable personality became the compass that he needed to navigate his life. He recalled her tenacity, her bravery, and her unyielding faith in the possibility of a brighter tomorrow. It turned out to be his only means of survival and a ray of light in the middle of the overwhelming gloom.

Within the confines of the city, Sofia's images started making their way outside the confines of their restricted nation. Her photographs of hopelessness and ruin, as well as savagery and defiance, struck a chord with people all around the world. They glared out from the front pages of newspapers and flashed on TVs, their unflinching reality causing a wave of outrage all around the world.

Despite this, the dictatorship did not show any sign of changing its attitude; its cruelty continued unabated, and their control over the city did not budge. They persisted in their harsh crackdown and cruel subjugation of the population. The city's soul looked to be crushed beneath the weight of despair as the crisis continued to worsen, and the city itself appeared to be falling apart.

The people's desperation transformed into a rage that would not be stilled, and the riots became more intense as a result. The air was heavy with the spirit of resistance, and the streets were filled with a clamor of defiance. The city was turned into a battlefield, and its residents were courageous soldiers who refused to submit to their rulers.

As the crisis grew worse, the atmosphere in Caracas took on an oppressive quality, with the noises of struggle, hunger, and resistance becoming ingrained in the city's very fabric. The usual sounds of the busy marketplaces and vibrant streets were replaced by the echo of gunfire, each burst serving as a gloomy punctuation point for their continuous tragedy.

A familiar sight on the sidewalks, Sofia could be seen walking about with her camera draped around her neck like an amulet. Her eyes were dry from looking through the viewfinder, and her fingers had become calloused from the continual clicking of the camera's shutter. Her images captured the city's sorrow, its utter hopelessness, and its fleeting, stubborn optimism.

One evening, she found herself in the middle of a brawl that had suddenly broken out for no apparent reason. She stood there, her pulse racing, while a sea of irate voices grew louder and louder around her. The demonstrators were only visible as shadows against the flames of the Molotov cocktail, and the echoes of their chants blended in with the sounds of the night.

This outburst of pent-up desperation was recorded by the lens of her camera as it was used by her. She noticed the fire reflected in the eyes of a young demonstrator, whose features were set in resolute purpose. The camera's shutter went off as a picture of an elderly lady appeared on the screen. The woman's feeble hands were firmly gripping a symbol of resistance, and her stubbornness was stronger than her wrinkles.

Alejandro sensed a shift in the atmosphere as he was confined in his cell at the same time. The guards were speaking in a frenzied whispering among themselves, and their eyes were wide with a terror that reflected the resolve that he had seen in the people in the past. He didn't need to hear it said for him to understand that the city had burst in rebellion, and that the people's desperation had turned into resistance.

He had a burst of optimism, a spark whose intensity was so strong that it was nearly painful. Even though he was not privy to the specifics, he saw Sofia in the thick of it, her energy as fiery and unending as the fires that were probably dancing on the streets. This notion, this link to the world outside his cell, made his captivity a bit more palatable, the frigid walls a little less oppressive than they would have been otherwise.

However, the harshness of the dictatorship was as impregnable as the concrete that encased him in his prison. An undertone to the rebellion that blazed outside the jail were the persistent tales of torture, disappearances, and the savage crackdowns.

Alejandro's spirit reverberated with the resistance that rocked the city outside, despite the walls that had been built around him to keep him captive. He pictured the streets being bathed in the harsh glow of burning tires, a chorus of voices rising against the tyranny, and electricity flashing in the air as a result of the uprising. In his thoughts, he was there with them, his soul free to roam, and his voice joining the booming cries for justice.

On a particular evening, the underlying sense of unease that was permeating his cell became more pronounced, and the guards' hushed conversations became increasingly agitated. He strained his hearing by pressing his ear against the cool stone and listening intently for any morsel of information that would provide him with a connection to the outside world. Hearing phrases like "riot," "crackdown," and "resistance" caused his heart to race with a feeling that was a cross between fear and hope.

Sofia painstakingly processed the photographs that she had taken inside of her cramped apartment, her heart breaking from the stories that the photographs depicted. Each shot was like hearing the heartbeat of a country on the verge of collapse as the chemicals mingled and whirled in the tray. The resulting photos were bleak depictions of conflict and defiance.

She stared at the picture of the elderly woman holding the placard; the lines on her face were the result of years of adversity, and the spark of unyielding defiance could be seen in her eyes. It was a demonstration of the tenacity and spirit of the people, especially in light of the atrocities that had been committed on them. When Sofia traced the image with her fingertips, she felt a tightening in her chest, and her fingers shook as they did so. She was aware that this photograph, along with a great number of others, constituted a record of their battle, and she was resolved to make that record known to the whole world.

In spite of the hopelessness that pervaded her environment, Sofia discovered a glimmer of optimism in the pictures of defiance that she observed. She saw fortitude in the faces of her people, a resolve that refused to bend down to the oppression that was intended to shatter them. She saw power in the faces of her people. She saw tenacity. She witnessed a nation that, in spite of its severe wounds, clung to hope and the idea of a brighter tomorrow. She saw a people that refused to give up.

Both Sofia and Alejandro found themselves engulfed in the whirlwind as the city was engulfed in the rising crisis, as the air grew heavy with the fragrance of tear gas and the echoes of gunfire, and as the city was swept up in the escalating crisis. Their personal narratives were intricately entwined with the overarching story of their country, and the hardships they faced were a microcosm of the bigger battle that was Venezuela.

In the middle of the night, Alejandro's cell was engulfed in a chilling stillness. All of the sounds, including the incessant hushing of voices, the shuffling of feet, and the clanging of metal on metal, were suddenly silenced. It seemed as though the institution had taken a deep breath before exhaling slowly in eager expectation. The atmosphere was thick with apprehension, and Alejandro felt its oppressive weight pushing down on him like a crushing burden.

After a few moments, the doors to his cell were violently wrenched open, and the sharp light from the hallway sliced through the pitch blackness like a sword. A number of guards could be seen standing against the light, their serious expressions obscured by the shadows cast by their bodies. One of them walked forward, and his words, which sounded like shards of ice, said, "It's time."

As Alejandro was being brought down a corridor, he could feel his heart thumping against his ribs and the anxiety of not knowing what was in store for him tightening its hold on his chest. Fear began to consume him as the guard's comments continued to play over and over in his head as he was led into a room that was sparsely furnished and barely illuminated.

During this moment, in the middle of Caracas, Sofia was standing on the edge of a rising throng while using her camera to capture real-time images of the escalation of the crisis. The atmosphere was thick with tension, a combustible mix of dread, wrath, and desperation that permeated everything. A symphony of resistance that resonated throughout the city was formed by the sound of protest shouts, sirens, and the occasional gunshot.

A little child, no older than ten, his diminutive form dwarfed by the throng of demonstrators, carrying a Venezuelan flag that fluttered boldly against the smoke grey sky while her camera clicked over a sight that would long be engraved in her memory: a young boy waving a Venezuelan flag that fluttered defiantly against the smoky grey sky. His eyes were reflecting the flames of blazing barricades, and his face was covered with soot from fighting. His mouth moved, and he chanted themes of freedom and justice that were far too profound for a child of his immature age.

It was eerie to see his innocent innocence set against the backdrop of such turbulent disobedience because the contrast was so stark. When Sofia hit the shutter button, her hands were shaking, and her heart was racing because of the significance of what she had shot.

This image, this tragic moment, epitomized the heart-wrenching truth of her country: the lost innocence and the stolen childhoods, sacrificed at the altar of the ambitious pursuit of power by a repressive dictatorship.

Sofia was astounded by the resiliency of her people, their indomitable spirit shining through the clouds of smoke and uncertainty. Despite the suffocating sadness, despite the carnage and turmoil, Sofia was astonished by the tenacity of her people. It was a demonstration of how relentlessly they fought for freedom and how steadfastly they believed in a future in which they would be liberated from the chains of oppression. And Sofia was aware that these moments, these tales of overcoming adversity, needed to be told to people all across the world.

Alejandro found himself in the uncomfortable position of having to face against a military trial. The atmosphere in the room reeked of icy justice. Each charge that was flung at him by the prosecutor, who was an authoritative guy dressed in military, landed like a blow. The accusations against him that rang throughout the room painted him as a traitor and accused him of "inciting riots," "spreading dissent," and "colluding with enemies of the state."

Although Alejandro's thoughts were spinning out of control, he did not cave in to the pressure of the allegations. He was a journalist, not a criminal; he was a voice for the voiceless, not a traitor. He clung to the knowledge that the truth was out there. However, the court did not pay attention to his pleadings since they had already reached their verdict long before he was brought in. The judgement of guilty put an end to any further consideration of his case and effectively sealed his destiny.

The news of Alejandro's arrest and subsequent detention quickly disseminated across the city. When Sofia heard the reports, it immediately caused her heart to sink. Her friend and comrade in the struggle for the truth, Alejandro, was being held up as an example to all of those who had the audacity to speak out against the administration. The knowledge hit her like a ton of bricks, and she found it difficult to take a breath because there was a lump in her throat, which made it difficult for her to swallow.

In spite of her anxiety, Sofia resolved to keep her word to herself and ensure that Alejandro's voice would not be stifled. She would make sure that everyone listened to his narrative. Her heart raced with redoubled resolve, and she made a solemn promise to herself that the world would never forget Alejandro. Venezuela would not be forgotten by the rest of the globe.

The situation continued to deteriorate as each day passed without resolution. The once-bustling marketplaces were now vacant, with rows of empty shelves replacing the colorful booths that had formerly occupied them. The majority of people found themselves constantly accompanied by hunger, their emaciated visage serving as a clear reminder of the catastrophe that had taken hold of the nation. A painful truth that threw a gloomy shade over the city was no longer a distant danger of starvation but rather had become a reality.

The ruthlessness of the administration was on full show throughout these dark days in the nation's history. Tear gas and rubber bullets were used on the demonstrators, turning their otherwise peaceful marches into scenes of mayhem and violence. Painful screams and the sound of sirens suddenly reverberated through the streets, which had before rung with the sound of laughing and active conversation. In before of Sofia and Alejandro's own eyes, the city that they had once known was vanishing, to be replaced by a dystopian environment that was filled with terror and pain.

Alejandro had his dignity taken from him by the officers in the prison, but they were unable to destroy his spirit. His determination became stronger by the day, and he never wavered in his commitment to the cause he was fighting for. He listened to the tales of injustice and tyranny that were told by his fellow inmates. These tales fueled the fires of his rebellion and inspired him to rebel. His resolve to bring the regime's crimes to light was strengthened with each new story he heard and injustice he saw, which only served to strengthen his resolve.

Alejandro was able to connect with the outside world by slipping secret messages to a guard who was sympathetic to his situation. He recorded the traumatic experiences of his fellow inmates, including a baker who was caught for failing to meet the mandated quota that he was required to deliver to the army, a student who was arrested for taking part in a demonstration, and an elderly man who was imprisoned for just expressing his criticism of the system. He laboriously put pen to paper, his tight calligraphy echoing the cramped constraints of his cage. He was confined to a small space.

During this time, Sofia was juggling her job as a photojournalist with her covert efforts to spread Alejandro's teachings. She felt as though she was walking a tightrope between the two. She was well aware of the danger she was putting herself in, namely that if she were caught, she would suffer the same fate as Alejandro, but she continued on nonetheless.

She made an effort to hold covert gatherings with members of the underground movement and made use of the contacts she had in order to disseminate Alejandro's notes. She stayed up all night converting the crumpled bits of paper into stories and then sent them off to various foreign news sites under a false name. Each article that was accepted for publication was like achieving a minor triumph; it was a ray of hope in the midst of the impending doom.

However, the human cost was substantial. Fear was Sofia's inseparable friend, and the unshakeable conviction that she was being observed and pursued never left her side. She saw shadows that looked sinister in every nook and cranny, and she heard rumors of a plot in every rustling. The atmosphere in her flat was more reminiscent of a fort than a home, and the camera she used felt more like a weapon than a tool. But she would not stop, and she was unable to stop either. Not while Alejandro was still being held captive, and not when her nation was on the verge of complete collapse.

Alejandro and Sofia both felt the weight of the hard truths of their new existence bearing down on them. Every day was a challenge to their fortitude, and every night was a fight against hopelessness.

Nevertheless, they persevered, drawing fortitude from the common goal they shared and the steadfast commitment they had to their cause.

However, as they progressed down their respective routes, the shadow of a dismal future became increasingly more apparent. The appearance of Venezuela was altering, with its characteristics transforming into something that was nearly indecipherable. They were staring into the abyss of hopelessness as it broke over them, casting its shadows far and wide.

During his time in jail, Alejandro rapidly fell into a terrible routine, which continued even after he was released. His days were filled with hard interrogations, little food, and the oppressive loneliness of his cell. He felt like he was suffocating. He was kept as a prisoner. In spite of the fact that the dictatorship inflicted the majority of its cruelty onto his body, it was his mind that was subjected to the greatest amount of anguish. There were times when he felt himself teetering on the brink of despair, but he held on to his resolution, and his determination served as a bulwark against the swelling tide of pessimism in his mind. When he found himself teetering on the brink of despair, he believed himself to be on the verge of giving up completely.

It wasn't only Alejandro who was having a hard time accepting the harshness of the situation; everyone was. Even Sofia, who had her own set of problems to deal with at the moment, was having trouble. The raw and unrefined shots that she has been shooting with her camera as of late are a long cry from the brightly colored landscapes and cheerful pictures that she used to take. Every single one of the shots was a harsh reminder of the dire situation that the country was in, and every single one of the frames was a dreadful picture of suffering.

In the midst of the mayhem, Sofia made contact with Marta, an old classmate of hers who had since gone on to become a nurse. Marta was an unlikely ally for Sofia. Because Marta's place of employment was the most important hospital in the city, she was able to observe firsthand the devastating impact that the crisis was having on the local population. She related stories of overcrowded rooms, limited medical supplies, and an alarming increase in the number of cases of malnutrition. She also mentioned an alarming increase in the number of cases of malnutrition. Marta's recollections were a depressing example of the human cost of the crisis, and as a consequence of Marta's explanations, Sofia developed a stronger sense of the hazardous condition that the country was in at the time.

As the predicament deteriorated, Sofia and Marta began to collaborate on various projects, and the fact that they were both dedicated to the same goal pulled them even closer. By enabling Sofia access to the hospital and allowing her to watch patients, Marta made it possible for Sofia to document the bleak truth of the current state of the healthcare system. The camera that was being carried by Sofia was a witness to the emaciated faces of children who were being starved, the tired eyes of overworked nurses, and the dismal feelings of families that had been torn apart by sickness and death.

As the country sank more into disorder, the personal costs of both Alejandro and Sofia continued to climb, which in turn led both of their circumstances to become increasingly challenging. Both Alejandro, who was held captive deep inside the depths of the regime's jail system, and Sofia, who placed her freedom in peril with each click of the shutter on her camera, were caught in the eye of the storm, and the crisis had a significant influence on both of their lives. Alejandro was held captive deep within the depths of the regime's jail system. Sofia put her freedom in jeopardy with each click of the shutter on her camera.

As time went on, the formerly prosperous nation remained on its path toward oblivion, and the deterioration of its condition accelerated with each passing day. Its streets, which were once alive with bustle, were now filled with the noises of demonstrations and the shouts of individuals who had given up hope for a better future. They watched in horror as the country that they loved was slowly converted into a place of shadows and echoes, while the citizens of that country were caught up in the grasp of an ever-worsening catastrophe.

Alejandro realized that as the days progressed into weeks, and then into months, he was completely absorbed in a world that was very different from the one he had previously known. The situation within the jail became a microcosm of the larger disaster that was unfolding beyond its gates. A gnawing sense of terror permeated the oppressive atmosphere, there was a severe lack of food, and tensions reached an all-time high. The prisoners, who were previously unique persons with well-defined identities, were reduced to nothing more than numbers, becoming faceless participants in a perverse game of survival.

In spite of the bleak circumstances, Alejandro was able to see signs of humanity. Because they were all going through the same ordeal, which is a powerful bonding mechanism, he became close with the other inmates. He listened to their accounts and gained an understanding of their life before to the catastrophe. There were men who had formerly enjoyed successful careers in other fields, students on the cusp of receiving their diplomas, and farmers caring to their property. They represented a cross-section of a society that had been ripped apart by the crisis. They were a mosaic representing the country's diverse population. Their stories broke my heart and served me a sobering reminder of the human cost of the crisis. However, they also served as a powerful illustration of the capacity of the human spirit to persevere in the face of hardship.

While everything was going on, Sofia was heading down a perilous road. Her profession as a photojournalist was becoming increasingly dangerous as the government cracked down on protests and other forms of opposition. She was driven off the streets, officials threatened her, and her residence was broken into. She persisted in spite of this, her work being driven by an unyielding sense of purpose, a compulsion to expose the hidden reality.

Her images were powerful and emotionally wrenching; they captured the people's real anguish as well as their resiliency. A child's skeleton that appears to be reaching for a handful of rice. An old lady, her eyes glazed over with the sorrow of loss, is seen cradling a photograph of her son, who has gone missing. A group of people joined together to show their resistance, raising their fists to be seen in shadow against the backdrop of a building that was on fire. The photographs taken by Sofia acted as a visual story of the catastrophe. They were unrelenting in their honesty and served as a plea for assistance in a world that had become deaf.

During the course of the crisis, both Alejandro and Sofia suffered a personal loss. In the middle of the medicine shortages, Alejandro was notified that his elderly mother had passed away. She had been unable to obtain any medication. He wept for her within the confines of his cell, the anguish of his loss made worse by the fact that he was locked up alone.

During a demonstration, Sofia saw the death of a colleague and a teacher who was a journalist. He was killed when he was caught in the crossfire and shot. Sofia grieved for him in private, his death serving as a sobering reminder of the dangers she was putting herself in and a stern warning of the potential repercussions her actions may have.

Nevertheless, despite the hopelessness of the situation, they continued to resist and battle. Their individual misfortunes served only to strengthen their commitment and their determination to hold the dictatorship accountable and expose the truth.

As the situation in the country deteriorated further, the stakes became an even greater concern. The pressure was increasing, not just from the inside but also from the outside. The iron fist of the regime was tightening its hold, but so was the resistance's hold. The situation was rapidly deteriorating, and the dawn of hopelessness had given way to a scorching noon heat. The crisis had reached a point of no return.

As the severity of the crisis increased, the severe conditions within the jail began to reflect those of the outside world. Carlos, Alejandro's cellmate and a former educator, was able to sneak in a pocket radio, and the two of them listened to the occasional broadcasts together. The broadcasts described in horrific detail the scope of the devastation that was occurring outside. People were in such a desperate state due to the widespread prevalence of starvation that they resorted to extreme means. It was reported that families were killing stray dogs and cats for their meat, that looting grocery shops turned into fatal fights, and that children who were malnourished fainted in classes.

Even with the bad news, Alejandro was able to cling to hope because to the radio. It reconnected him to the world he had been torn away from and gave him an understanding of the harsh realities that his nation was going through at the time. Alejandro desperately hung on to every syllable that emanated from the little speaker as the days stretched into weeks. He listened to the tragedy that was taking on beyond the boundaries of his realm, the violence that the dictatorship meted out to the populace. Each broadcast strengthened his resolve to persevere, to live, and, if the gods would have it, to fight back.

Even Sofia was beginning to feel the effects of the crisis, but in a manner that was unique to her. Her line of work was risky from the beginning, but it had recently become extremely hazardous. She took her camera with her whenever she went outdoors, and she was very aware that each time she did so, it was possible that she would never return. The government's assault on the media had been stepped up, and as a result, more of her colleagues were either going missing or winding up dead. Despite this, she was adamant about bringing awareness to the horrors that were being done. The entire globe needed to be informed. Her camera served as both a weapon and a shield, and it also served as her voice.

In spite of the severity of the situation, Sofia was able to convey in each photograph the resiliency and bravery of her people. She took pictures of the riots that were taking place in the middle of Caracas, the hopeless lines that formed in front of the decreasing food banks, and the quiet vigils that were held for the people who had vanished. Her images were unfiltered and distressing; they were a searing plea for assistance from a nation that was in the grips of a nightmare.

While navigating the perilous streets, Sofia realized that she was also being drawn into the core of the resistance movement. Her work had attracted the attention of a covert group of revolutionaries who were working toward the destruction of the regime. They respected her bravery and thought that the contribution she could make to their cause would be amplified by her job. This was a precarious situation for Sofia to be in. If you were involved with the rebels, the government would classify you as a major target because of your affiliation with them. Despite this, she saw hope for a better Venezuela and was motivated to work toward it because she recognized the possibility for change.

Her participation in the uprising increased the depth of her immersion into the tragedy that Venezuela had become. She emerged as a key figure in the revolution, acting not just as a witness but also as a chronicler and a spokesperson. Her images started to portray increasingly heartbreaking stories, such as the grim resolve on the faces of the rebels, the despair yet stubborn eyes of the regular residents who were being pushed to their limits, and the fading beauty of a country that was gasping for breath.

While Sofia was documenting the uprising, Alejandro was going through a journey within the walls of the prison that was quite similar to hers. His hopelessness gave way to a grim determination to fight, to live, and maybe even to fight back from the inside. The lessons he learned about resistance, patience, and the unconquerable human spirit from his cellmate Carlos began to form his own determination. These teachings helped him better understand the indomitable human spirit. Alejandro was brought into the prison's underground network of insurgents by Carlos, a former educator who was incarcerated for political reasons. Within the very core of the regime's apparatus, a clandestine uprising was quietly taking shape with the help of hushed conversations and secret signals.

Alejandro may have been physically restricted behind the prison walls, but his spirit remained unchained the entire time. Even though the lack of food caused him to lose weight, his will to succeed only got greater as time went on. He started helping his fellow inmates by using his medical skills to cure wounds and diseases using the little resources that were available. This helped him win their respect and, more significantly, their trust. Because of his courage and doggedness, Alejandro became an inspiration to a good number of his fellow inmates, and word of his tenacity quickly travelled through the dismal halls of the jail.

The cries for liberty of the people reverberated not just through the deserted streets of the once-bustling cities but also off the old and filthy walls of the jail cells. The images taken by Sofia and the indomitable attitude that Alejandro exhibited were two sides of the same coin; they were different yet parallel narratives of a nation that was under assault.

In her own unique way, Sofia was engaged in a conflict of a like nature on the surface. Her images were published by worldwide news organizations, which drew the attention of people all over the world. The stark and terrifying photos that she caught were worth more than a thousand words each, and they pierced the hearts of everyone who saw them. And even as the government persisted in downplaying the severity of the crisis, Sofia's images stood as a testament to the grim truth of the situation.

In a world that was getting more chaotic and sadder by the day, Sofia found some semblance of order in the viewfinder of her camera lens. The focal point of her camera brought out in startling relief the humanity that was present in the situation, which stood in stark contrast to the general mayhem. She searched for tiny moments of compassion, love, resistance, and hope amidst the awful scenes of misery and violence that surrounded her. She found her strength in the tenacity of her people, namely in their resolve to suffer injustice and fight against it.

In one of these instances, a riot broke out in the heart of Caracas because people were upset about the price of food. Sofia was able to capture on tape a group of women who were defiantly standing against the military police and clutching the barrels of the guns that were pointed at them with their bare hands. It was clear in the moms' eyes that they were watching over their little children with an unwavering maternal zeal that could not be shaken. When Sofia clicked the button that activated the camera's shutter, she immortalized that instance of unrestrained bravery for the entire world to see.

Alejandro was confined to the jail while all of this was going on, and he was forced to watch as his fellow inmates perished as a result of the brutal treatment they suffered from their guards. Nevertheless, in spite of the indescribable anguish, he recognized fortitude in their unmovable spirit. They would not bend under the strain, nor would they shatter when the pressure was applied. During the course of the conflict, Alejandro took it upon himself to converse with them, to encourage them, and to treat their wounds in order to keep their spirits alive.

Because of his time spent inside, Alejandro developed into a decisive leader throughout the course of his career. His words had the potential to inspire hope, his bravery served as a guiding light for them, and his medical knowledge was their final hope for survival. His words had the ability to inspire hope. Alejandro was unable to stop what was going to happen when there was a lack of food and medical supplies, but he refused to let his fellow hostages die in a shameful fashion. This was despite the fact that he was unable to stop what was going to happen. In the midst of such insurmountable challenges, Alejandro developed his own unique style of defiance and his own strategy for combating the opposition.

It seemed as though Sofia and Alejandro's lives were merging as the tension increased both inside and outside the jail where they were both being held. In spite of the fact that they were involved in distinct fights, both of them were striving toward the same goal, which was the freedom of Venezuela. Both are driven by an unyielding passion to combat the deteriorating situation, to document it, and to be witnesses to it. This determination motivates them both to write about it.

Their resistance reverberated across the country like a faraway drumbeat, and it was clear that they were not going to give in. The photos of Sofia have sparked outrage and empathy all around the world, which has contributed to an increase in the amount of pressure that is being put on the dictatorship of Maduro. The other inmates at the facility were given a reason to have hope as a result of Alejandro's stoic resistance behind the walls of the jail, which in turn prompted the guards and wardens to become more alarmed. In spite of the fact that the conflict was not yet over, the framework for a resistance movement had been established.

The most difficult time of year for anyone living in Venezuela was the scorching summer of that year. The country was a ticking time bomb, and its citizens were on the edge, torn between the crushing pain of their current situation and the yearning desire for a better tomorrow. The country was a time bomb waiting to go off. The riots became routine because pent-up animosity constantly bubbled to the surface in the form of violence and killing. The once-mighty Orinoco no longer appeared to be the backbone of a thriving nation; rather, it mirrored the unrest and instability taking place throughout the country it traversed. This was so because Venezuela is in the river's path.

Despite all that was happening, Alejandro's voice could be heard throughout the prison, inspiring hope in the other inmates. However, there was a cost associated with his sway over events. The guards in charge of maintaining order in the prison started seeing him as a danger, someone who could set off a riot among the inmates. However, he remained dedicated even as he spent more and more dangerous days behind prison.

On the other hand, Sofia kept clicking photos of the mayhem unfolding around her. Her pictures were a portal for the world to see the atrocities committed by the regime and a light for her people to follow. The crimes committed against her people were committed by the regime. Her photographs became a form of covert resistance, and her camera evolved into a weapon.

As tear gas is thrown into the streets, Sofia is there with her camera to capture this moment in a nation's history. Even in the dark and confined space of his cell, Alejandro's defiance is claimed to shine brilliantly, and his spirit has not been shattered. Though the roads they choose are loaded with peril, there remains a glimmer of hope that things may be different and that change is possible. Their histories have not been fully revealed, nor have all of their contributions to the shaping of the nation's fate been uncovered.

They are a shining light at the worst hour for their country, exemplifying the resolute will of the Venezuelan people. They are a shining representation of the perseverance of the Venezuelan people.

The last curtain has been drawn, setting the stage for further struggle, new obstacles, and perhaps some hope.

CHAPTER 4 "GATHERING SHADOWS"

The persistent haze of smoke that covered the sky above Caracas was a visible sign of the turmoil that was taking place on the city's streets. In spite of this, it seemed as though life in the city was trying to continue in rebellious bursts of color and energy despite the circumstances. Children were laughing as they played football in the tiny passageways, and the rich sounds of salsa music could be heard escaping from behind closed doors. In the background, the perfume of freshly cooked arepas filled the air. In the midst of mayhem and disarray, this place was a city and a country doing its best to maintain some kind of order.

Nearby Plaza Bolivar, in an unremarkable and somewhat unassuming structure, Sofia was processing her images. The harsh chemicals helped bring to life the terrible reality of the discontent, rebellion, and despair that her people were experiencing. It was in this gloomy chamber, bathed in the warm red glow of the safe light, that she finally came to terms with the seriousness of what she had been chronicling.

When I was in the middle of one of these particularly intense sessions, there was a tap at the door. A guy stood in the open air, the harsh sunlight of Venezuela and the numerous challenges of life having left their marks on his face. He introduced himself as Antonio and stated that they had worked together and been friends in the past. Antonio was now on the run after breaking out of the prison and asking for assistance.

Sofia was neither shocked or appalled by Antonio's accounts of the atrocities that occurred at the jail. She was aware of the rumors and had witnessed the dismal truth reflected in the expressions of the detainees' relatives. The thing that really took her by surprise was when Antonio brought up Alejandro, the doctor, who was the symbol of hope for the convicts. The guy whose bravery and audacity were shaking the very foundations of the institution was named Alejandro. Because they both opposed the government in the same way, Sofia and Alejandro developed a strong connection with one another.

After Antonio had departed, Sofia continued to think about what he had said. It was as if the suffering of the prisoners and the hopeless optimism in Alejandro's eyes were following her everywhere she went. After that, she had an epiphany about what she had to do. Her photographs were necessary in order to portray Alejandro's narrative. They needed to inform the outside world about the atrocities that were taking on behind the confines of the jail, they needed to bring the truth to light, and they needed to water the seeds of revolt. Her thoughts started to formulate a strategy, one that was perilous but also powerful; it was a strategy that had the potential to drastically alter Venezuela's destiny.

In the meantime, Alejandro was taken from the musty confines of his cell and placed in the glaring sunlight of the yard outside the prison. It was as if the light were searing his eyes, serving as a jarring reminder that there was a world outside the stone and steel. The officials in charge of the correctional facility were starting to feel uneasy about his influence, but they were unable to stop him. The struggle of his fellow detainees and the expanding desolation outside fueled the fire of resilience that already burned within his heart and provided further fuel for it.

Alejandro's hands were able to find some peace and comfort in their labor, even behind the bars of his cell. He was able to keep his attention on the task at hand and his spirits up in spite of the depressing atmosphere around him. These were the instruments of his defiance: a makeshift stethoscope, crude bandages, and a notebook stuffed with case narratives. He wasn't simply a doctor to the other people who were locked up with him; to them, he was a symbol of the unyielding resistance that refused to go out. He was a light of hope.

While Alejandro worked hard to bring healing to a place that was designed to tear down the human soul, Sofia began her perilous mission on the outside. She traveled into the shanty communities, the barrios, and the marketplaces with Antonio as her guide, capturing the human face of the crisis as well as the raw spirit of their battle. Her camera, which never shied away from a challenge, actively sought out sharp contrasts, simmering wrath, and forlorn hope.

The first time that Sofia and Alejandro's paths crossed was at one of these rallies, which had descended into violence by the time they were there. In order to aid with the medical emergency, Alejandro, who was out on a brief parole, found himself knee-deep in the mayhem, his doctor's coat splattered with the blood of the demonstrators.

As a result of being trapped in the middle of the chaos, Sofia found herself in very close proximity to Alejandro. He stood in the thick of the mass of bodies, his hands a jumble, but his expression remained resolute and unwavering. She watched as he triaged the wounded, his face set in grim resolve as he kept his hands steady despite the chaos that was going on around him. Sofia found herself fascinated by Alejandro despite the yelling and screaming, the flash of tear gas, and the gunfire that was going on. Her heart was filled with the reverberation of his energy, his resiliency, and his pure humanity. After a brief lapse in memory, she remembered to pick up her camera and refocused it, this time on Alejandro.

Alejandro could feel the pressure of a look on him even though he was in the middle of his task. When he looked up, he saw Sofia's eyes looking back at her from the other side of the chaos. He saw a reflection of his own resolve and resistance in her, and she served as a mirror for him. It seemed to her that her camera, which was a weapon of truth, was less of an intrusion and more of an ally. The quick and intense connection that they had marked the beginning of a collaboration that would eventually challenge the fundamental foundation on which the system was built.

In the middle of the tumult of that fateful day, the paths of Sofia and Alejandro linked and then wrenched apart, thereby putting in motion a destiny that none of them could have predicted. After seeing Alejandro's unwavering bravery, Sofia found herself becoming more sympathetic to the cause he was fighting for. Every one of her postures reverberated with his uncompromising energy, fanning the coals of defiance that burned within her heart.

In the meantime, Alejandro was pulled back into the bowels of the jail, and this time his heart was burdened with more than simply the misery of his fellow inmates. The recollection of Sofia's look, her unspoken determination, turned into a wellspring of power and served as a guidepost for him even in the most desolate parts of his imprisonment.

As the days went by, the simmering discontent eventually erupted into open revolt. In light of the fact that her photographs were now carrying the weight of Alejandro's defiance, Sofia started taking greater risks and went further into the core of the regime's violence. She took pictures of the riot police, the food queues, the slums, and the faces of the people there; there were so many faces that showed signs of sorrow, resiliency, and resolve.

In the meantime, Alejandro was transforming into a symbol of resistance and strength as he was confined to his jail cell. His actions and his steadfast spirit were talked about in hushed tones and relayed around the grapevine that flowed through the depths of the prison. His activities were praised for their consistency. He became a folk hero for those who were oppressed as a result of the stories that spread far and wide about his bravery.

Simultaneously, Sofia's work was making headway and gathering traction. The pictures that she shot, each one filled with Alejandro's energy and her own will, began to circulate clandestinely among the people of the town. A spark of revolt was lit among the populace as a result of these unvarnished, unedited views into their everyday struggle. The formidable combination of Sofia's camera and Alejandro's unyielding willpower stirred up the waters of a hush-hush tsunami that was just beginning to swell.

The repressive dictatorship, on the other hand, continued to be unaware of the mounting tide of resistance. The cogs of oppression spun unceasingly, bringing down everything in their path and leaving nothing standing. It was a troubling moment for Venezuela, a period in which even the faintest expression of disapproval might result in severe repercussions. Even though Sofia and Alejandro faced an extremely difficult situation, not one of them gave up.

Sofia persisted in braving the dangerous streets, and her camera continued to capture the harsh realities of their lives. While everything was going on, Alejandro worked tirelessly within the limitations of his prison to provide his fellow detainees encouragement and solace.

As we went from one terrible reality to the next, life gradually began to take on an odd quality. As she made her way over the crumbling landscape of Venezuela, Sofia seemed to be moving through a waking dream the entire time. Every time she touched the shutter button on her camera, it was like a heartbeat, a throb of life in the midst of all of the death and decay that had become their daily food. She was able to capture these moments of life and bring them back to them later. The most stunning feature of their conflict was how her camera was able to capture the unfettered and wild spirit of humans that refused to be controlled. This was the most important component of their struggle.

In the meantime, Alejandro's cell had transformed into a fortress and a safe haven for him to retreat to in times of crisis. Within such depressing and suffocating constraints, he provided a glimpse of hope and lit a flame of insurrection. His actions and his spirit left an imprint on those dirty passageways, and they echoed with the optimism that a revolution was on the horizon. His actions left an impression on those filthy hallways.

Despite this, the authoritarian government's grip on power tightened to the point that it resembled a chokehold with each passing day. The voices of those who opposed the government were silenced, and even the slightest bit of resistance was mercilessly suppressed. Even though it was a sign of hope, Alejandro's cell was a dangerous place to be even if it was a positive signal. The possibility of being found out and punished loomed large and menacingly like a cloud in the sky.

The fact that Sofia and Alejandro were not in the same location at the same time did not prevent them from being unified in their fight. As more and more people saw Sofia's photos, a growing spirit of resistance and fury developed. When Alejandro was first made aware of the outside world, he felt an immediate surge of pride and a rekindled sense of purpose for his life. Their connection, which was not verbalized but was still powerful, served as a beacon and guided them through the gloom by illuminating the path forward.

The sun was about to set on the skyline of Caracas, which produced long, spooky shadows that seemed to imitate the despair and resolve that were now inscribed on the faces of the city's citizens. These shadows were produced as the sun was beginning to set on the skyline of Caracas. It was clear that Sofia had a good grasp of the idea. In her shot, she was able to capture the remarkable contrast between the peaceful sunset and the severe surroundings. It was a remarkable photograph that functioned both as a depiction of their adversity and as a testimony to their ability to persevere in the face of adversity.

Inside his cell again, Alejandro began planning a modest but massive uprising. It all began with hushed conversations, secret gatherings, and barely perceptible rebellion. Many of his fellow inmates saw for the first time a glimmer of optimism, a glimpse of a future not clouded by terror. Their unsuspecting leader, Alejandro, came to personify this bravado, a ray of light in a world of darkness.

Meanwhile, Sofia handled the complex political climate with maturity beyond her years. Her pictures quickly became a symbol of their struggle, appearing as audacious graffiti on walls and improvised billboards. They displayed an unvarnished reflection of their anguish for all to see. More and more people were interested in their cause as Sofia exposed the truth via her lens.

Although Alejandro and Sofia's lives took different directions, they had a same goal. They started a revolt not merely against the repressive dictatorship, but also against the paralyzing terror that had possessed them. It was a revolution of hope, guided by the bravery of the downtrodden and the resolve of two courageous souls.

The night became darker and the shadows longer. Still, there was a glimmer of hope, a revolution in the making in the shadows. The voyage was filled with risk and uncertainty, but they persisted, spurred on by their unyielding resolve and the hope of a brighter tomorrow.

Their journeys went in different directions, but they had a goal. Although the odds were stacked against them, they kept fighting. There was a glimmer of hope, a promise of a fresh dawn, even in the depths of despair as the night grew darker and the shadows grew closer.

As the evenings became darker and colder, it seemed as if the shadows were trying to tell Alejandro and Sofia something. The rumors spread a message of strength and solidarity, rebellion against the authorities. The hesitant leader of the jail uprising, Alejandro, kept the spirit of defiance alive by feeding and tending to it with all his power and will. His other convicts, who had previously been hopeless and despondent, began to dare to hope again. For the first time, they were able to see a future beyond the filthy bars of their cages. Alejandro's defiant attitude sparked their latent bravery, inspiring them to join him in his fight for independence.

Meanwhile, Sofia was out doing her own thing in the world. Each new set of images she took was an exposé of the savagery of the dictatorship that had oppressed them. They were shocking reminders of the people's situation, galvanizing them into action. With each snap of her camera, Sofia exposed the lies buried behind the propaganda. A visual monument to the regime's misdeeds, her brave graffiti on the city walls galvanized more people to their cause.

But the crisis did reach Sofia. She had to rely on her wits to get through the perilous environment, which presented new challenges every day. But she would not allow her determination to be thwarted. Sofia viewed the difficulty as an obstacle she must conquer on her way to success. Because she had faith in her camera's ability to inspire action and rally the downtrodden, she kept taking pictures of them while they fought.

Alejandro and Sofia shared a great bond despite not being physically close. The prison walls kept them apart, but their common goals and struggles brought them closer together. Each person found inspiration in the other's fortitude, and their fighting souls joined as one. Their disobedience and acts sparked a wave of revolt that spread throughout the city and even behind the prison gates.

The night grew darker and the shadows thicker, but a revolution was stirring in the darkness. A revolution sparked by the determination of two people and propelled by the hopes of an oppressed population. A glimmer of light pierced through the night, suggesting the arrival of a new day.

There was never any peace throughout the night in Caracas. Lullabies that rocked the city to sleep were the rumble of distant gunfire, the moans of empty stomachs, and the sobs of mothers who had lost too much. Alejandro and Sofia were able to find harmony in their lives despite the constant discord they were exposed to.

Alejandro became a symbol of defiance in the prison's central courtyard. Once a symbol of his captivity, his cell has become a center of clandestine operations. In secret, crude yet effective homemade weapons were developed. The air was thick with the palpable eagerness of those who had heard the rumors of escape plans. The guys in Alejandro's cell block, from all walks of life, came together to support him because of their common pain. The eyes, which had been dead before, glowed with a renewed resolve. Alejandro's courage and determination revitalized their weary spirits.

But Sofia was fighting a far more obvious foe. Graffiti was her war cry and her camera was her weapon. Each photograph served as an indictment of the government, and each wall was a declaration of defiance. She walked through the desolate streets of Caracas at night, leaving her artwork as a form of protest at every intersection. Sofia took comfort in her defiance even as anxiety and doubt threatened to overwhelm her. Her bravery echoed across the city's deserted avenues and byways, and she had become a spokesperson for the voiceless.

With each passing day, Alejandro and Sofia's lives were more intricately entwined in a dance of resistance and hope. They shared a desire for liberty and fair treatment. They saw in one another the fortitude to persevere, struggle, and stand up against. And they discovered an unexplainable solace, a peculiar sense of kinship, in their common ordeal.

Even though it was late, the night was noisy. Rebellion rumors were spreading and became more brazen. The previously aimless darkness foretold of a new day. A new day had begun, one in which Alejandro and Sofia could proudly display the fruits of their resistance and suffering. The day they had been waiting for, driven by an unyielding opposition spirit and a common hope for a better Venezuela.

In the midst of the catastrophe, Alejandro and Sofia found comfort in one another. There were brief respites, times of shared laughter and meaningful chats despite the impending doom. They saw a Venezuela liberated from dictatorship, with a population whose daily rhythm was set not by the need to scrounge for food and water but by the rich diversity of its culture and landscape. The revolt took on new meaning as they experienced these moments of joy together. The goal had shifted from simple survival to the restoration of their legitimate way of life.

Alejandro began to feel an unusual calm in Sofia's company among all the hidden planning and discussions. The warmth she exuded was a welcome contrast to the harshness of their situation. Her positive attitude was contagious, and her dogged persistence shone like a lighthouse, giving him reason to believe even on the darkest days. He found himself sharing his deepest thoughts and feelings with her, including his hopes, goals, and regrets. Alejandro, the rebel commander known for his stoicism, broke down in front of Sofia and discovered strength he didn't know he had.

In exchange, Alejandro's perseverance served as an inspiration to Sofia. His fortitude and determination caused her to recall the reasons she had chosen to capture this moment with her camera. The connection they had shone like a beacon in the otherwise bleak reality of their lives. Sofia viewed Alejandro as a collaborator, friend, and companion. He was the one consistency in the mayhem, the one ray of light in the darkness. This faith was the driving force behind Sofia's defiance.

The concept of a united opposition germinated in these private times, amid whispered murmurs and shared hopes. It wasn't only about getting away from the prison or the graffiti. It was a rallying cry for everyone to take up arms against the dictatorship. With the help of Sofia's bold artwork, Alejandro would hatch a plot to start a revolution in Venezuela.

But even as they daydreamed and plotted, darkness was creeping closer. Daily, the regime's repressive measures became more extreme and brazen. Time was of the essence in this fight against terror. Alejandro and Sofia understood the urgency of the situation and the need to take swift action for the future of Venezuela and their hopes and goals.

As the love between Alejandro and Sofia deepened, so did the opposition. Their allies were systematically eliminated as the regime's iron grip increased, turning the streets into battlefields. The weight of the rebels' cause became heavier on Alejandro with each one of them who fell. Each defeat served as a chilling reminder of the price of their revolt, a reminder that only served to harden his determination.

At the same time, Sofia began taking more in-depth documentation of their fight, which managed to capture the hopelessness, fortitude, and humanity even within the chaos. Her images were now also about the courageous individuals who were resisting the regime's brutality. It was about the grim resolve on Alejandro's face as he rallied his fellow rebels, the rebellious graffiti that covered the city's walls, the camaraderie that resulted from sharing little food, and the steely resolve in the eyes of those who were prepared to confront the dictatorship head-on.

The paths of their separate universes were beginning to converge. Their uprising had evolved into a fight for survival and redemption. Now, not only did they have a common foe, but also a common goal: victory. Even so, they were aware of how risky the road ahead was and how high the stakes would be if they failed.

The difficulties they faced lengthened and darkened with the passage of time. Alejandro spent his evenings plotting and scheming, recruiting supporters, and probing the government for vulnerabilities. On the other hand, Sofia's images spoke volumes about their cause, stirring the people and stoking the flames of their resistance; she was the voice of their uprising.

The dictatorship, meanwhile, was observing the two rebels as they plotted and planned, their presence becoming darker and darker like a shadow. Heavy footsteps echoed louder through the dark alleys, and a greater sense of foreboding permeated the night. The possibility of being found out threw a long, ominous shadow over Alejandro and Sofia's preparations. They needed to move quickly if they were to realize their goal of a free Venezuela.

As tensions rose, the importance of the coordinated uprising's preparations became clear. Every second of calm was priceless, and every gaze they exchanged strengthened their commitment to one another. They were only two people up against a system, but they were armed with hope and determination. There was a swell of darkness, but there was also a swell of rebels. The scene had been set. The uprising was just about to start.

Knowing that even a minor misstep might have disastrous consequences, Alejandro spent endless hours researching, planning, and practicing for an insurrection. His mind was continuously racing with possible strategies and countermeasures as he analyzed the regime's motions, strengths, and vulnerabilities. Maps and scrawled notes, schematics of government buildings and probable hideouts, all covered the walls of his apartment, turning it into a war room.

There was a palpable sense of foreboding in the air as the clock ticked away the minutes till their uprising. They were fully aware of the dangers of the expedition they had begun. However, they had an unwritten pact: they wouldn't let fear control them. They couldn't afford the luxury of fear.

While this was happening, Sofia's camera was recording the developing story. She gave the globe a glimpse of their deteriorating nation through her photography. Secret meetings, stubborn looks, and indications of a growing uprising joined the previously seen pictures of starving children, repressed citizens, and abusive military. Her pictures had become emblems of defiance and resistance for those who were too timid to take up arms, and they had been used to narrate tales of bravery and fortitude to those who were ready to join their cause.

Sofia and Alejandro entered a poorly lit room to see a group of people crowded around a makeshift table in the dead of night. Tension hung heavy in the room, and the dim light from the lone lamp cast shadows on the gloomy features around the table. Alejandro spread out a map, his fingers following the maze of streets with furious resolve in his gaze.

Alejandro's voice took on an unusual weight as he said, "Tomorrow, we take a stand," and the weight of his words sank deep into the hearts of the rebels in attendance. Sofia watched Alejandro, her breath catching as she realized the magnitude of their imminent revolution and her pulse beating in time with the clock.

Their war cry reverberated in the hushed whispers and resolute nods as the night progressed and plans were completed and roles were allocated. The sun was just peeking over the horizon, throwing long shadows through the holes in the walls that served as a chilling reminder of the massive conflict that lay ahead.

Looking into her eyes, Alejandro felt both fear and resolution in Sofia. Their resolve was as firm as their cause, and they were prepared to act. The revolt they sowed had grown into towering trees throwing foreboding shadows, a portent of doom for Venezuela. The darkness was no longer a sign of hopelessness, but rather of their dogged determination.

Alejandro got up from the table without a word, his gaze never leaving Sofia's. He walked over to the dusty record player in the far corner of the room. Alejandro extended his hand to Sofia as the faint notes of a forgotten tune floated through the air. For a little second, they had forgotten their worries about the impending uprising and the specter of hopelessness. They were no longer revolutionary soldiers on the verge of battle, but rather a man and a woman dancing by the light of an old lantern, the beat of their hearts in sync with their hopes and desires.

With each maneuver, they were making an invisible declaration of support for the common cause. Sofia laid her head on Alejandro's shoulder, letting the music take her to a place where they were neither warriors nor lovers, but rather free spirits whose hearts beat to the same pace and whose dreams for a better Venezuela were intertwined like the rhythm of their dance.

Alejandro and Sofia broke away from their dance as the sun rose, coloring the morning sky with shades of red and orange, their look acknowledging the momentary peace they had found in one other's embrace. They had reached an unspoken agreement in silence. It was a brief calm in their often-turbulent lives, a wonderful interlude that gave them hope for the future.

Sofia saw a new side of Alejandro in the early light, one in which he was not just a fierce revolutionary but also a caring guy who deeply cared about his nation. And to him, she was more than simply a brave lady; she represented renewal for their tired country. These shared experiences of vulnerability strengthened their friendship, the strands of their developing attachment tangled with the roots of their rebellion.

The dawn, however, brought sobering thoughts. The ticking of the clock replaced the thump of the record player, and the twirl of shadows gave way to the glare of early morning sunlight. They were fighting not just the repressive government but also the passage of time.

They went back to doing their own jobs, but now felt more connected than ever. And as the night lengthened, their resolve only got stronger. They were prepared for the oncoming revolution. Together, they would confront it, just as they had overcome their own anxieties. Daylight was slowly breaking, and the growing shadows emphasized the resolve on their features.

Alejandro and Sofia's relationship strengthened over the next few days, becoming a stable pillar in the midst of their otherwise turbulent circumstances. Along with their common goal came late-night confidantes, lingering stares, and hints of plans. As they spoke and sat together, they grew closer. The uprising that had brought them together was now serving as background to their developing romance.

However, love during the revolutionary period was a stormy affair. There were hastily arranged meetings under the cover of darkness, coded messages, and whispered chats. Every second counted, and everything said between them was kept secret.

The secret letters they exchanged twirled around their emotions and layers of revolutionary zeal. Alejandro's shaky penmanship covered many pages, outlining strategies and procedures but also peppering them with private messages to Sofia filled with love and excitement.

Each letter that Sofia received was a link to the guy who had come to mean so much to her. She would spend hours reading them and touching the letters to "feel" his handwriting. Their love developed through these quiet conversations, these private times.

The closer they became, the more pressing their goal became. The news of the uprising went across the city, seeping into every nook and cranny. There were rumors of a revolution spreading through the busy marketplaces and winding streets. There was a perceptible tension in the air, like the buildup to a storm's climax. The uprising they had been plotting was almost ready to begin.

Through it all, Alejandro and Sofia were the pivot, the unseen orchestrators of a revolt that dwarfed both of them. Once a symbol of decline and tyranny, the city now boiled over with an unsettling agitation. The shadows were lengthening and deepening, becoming the silhouette of an impending uprising.

There was excitement, anxiety, and optimism in the world beyond their safe haven. They sought refuge in one other's arms at their secret encounters, their love a haven from the storm outside. Their love story, set against the backdrop of a country on the verge of upheaval, was only one thread in the fabric of their lives.

One night, on the eve of what would be their first act of disobedience, Sofia and Alejandro found themselves on the rooftop of an old, dilapidated building overlooking the center of Caracas. The structure was located in a dangerous neighborhood. The lights of the city twinkled like stars, and the smell of imminent precipitation filled the air. The stillness of the city was broken by the mutterings of those involved in the uprising.

Alejandro finally broke the quiet while his voice was shaking slightly. "Tomorrow, we will begin traveling down a road from which there is no turning back. Because of you, Sofia, our lives will never be the same.

"I know," Sofia murmured, her voice barely audibles above the thumping rhythm of the city's heartbeat in the background. But this is a war we have to win, Alejandro. Our opportunity to put things in the proper perspective."

Alejandro whirled around to face her, his eyes intent and determined as he did so. "There is something I need to talk to you about, Sofia," the speaker said. He stopped, drawing in a full breath as he struggled to resist the impulse to grab her and hold her in his arms. "I want you to know that I love you regardless of what happens tomorrow," the text reads.

There was complete silence between them. The fear, hope, and love that were in Sofia's eyes were mirrored in his eyes as she gazed up at him. "I love you too, Alejandro."

Alejandro drew Sofia into his arms just as the first drops of rain began to fall. As the rain became steadily heavier, the metropolis that was in front of them began to become a complex pattern of lights and shadows. However, despite the impending storm, the warmth that they shared remained unshaken. Their vows of silence, which were then confirmed with a long, drawn-out kiss, resounded into the night.

On the eve of the uprising, the couple had a love that was as intense as the fight that was about to be waged against them. In the midst of the darkening clouds brought on by the approaching storm and the oncoming rebellion, Sofia and Alejandro had discovered an unbreakable love for one another. Their emotions, which had before been burdened by the anguish of their homeland, were now filled with love and defiance. At the break of a new day, not only would there be an uprising, but also the resolute determination of two hearts that were bound together by love and obligation would become clear.

The revolt was about to happen. The uprising, which was also their uprising, was prepared to shake off the gloom of hopelessness. And yet, despite everything that was going on, love had managed to prevail. As the last lines are written, the beginning of a brand-new age quickly approaches. The road that lies ahead is one that is lined with effort, hope, and the unyielding will of love.

CHAPTER 5 "SEEDS OF REBELLION"

Alejandro awakened to a day that was unlike any other when the first rays of dawn broke through the darkness of the squalor that pervaded the neighborhood. This was the day that the downtrodden would no longer use silence as their primary mode of communication. This was the day that talk would turn into deeds, when whispers would become roars, and when shadows would emerge into the light.

Alejandro was able to make out the features of his other comrades in the dim light of their makeshift headquarters, which consisted of an abandoned warehouse tucked amid deteriorating buildings. Their eyes gleamed with a defiance that belied their thin looks and the shabby garments that they wore. They were men and women, young and elderly. They were the oppressed, the disillusioned, and the sufferers of a once affluent nation's fall from grace. They were the victims of a once prosperous nation's fall from grace. Nevertheless, the beat of defiance reverberated inside their very beings; it was a common cadence that held them together as one.

Because Alejandro had previously held a position of authority in the military, he found himself in a position of leadership during the crisis. Everyone in the group looked to him for direction and direction in strategy. He started organizing the uprising with the tenacity of a soldier and the loyalty of a real patriot in his heart. His military outfit, which had once been pristine and now appeared old and torn, served as a continual reminder of a past that appeared to be nothing more than a faraway dream. In spite of this, the raging fire of defiance that burned inside him stood in sharp contrast to the hopelessness that had become ingrained in the very fabric of their existence.

In the meantime, Sofia discovered that she was cast in the role she had always envisioned playing, albeit under circumstances she could not have foreseen. Sofia became the voice of the uprising, using her voice as a weapon and her pen as a shield. She wrote of their hardship, their hopes, and the impending rebellion in their community. Her remarks, which were resolute and uncompromising, made their way into the core of the city, igniting a flame of rebellion in even the most downtrodden individuals. She wrote from the epicenter of the movement, and the words that she chose to use painted vivid pictures of their suffering, their determination, and the impending upheaval.

The reporting that Sofia did became a guiding light for them and a rallying cry for individuals who had the audacity to imagine a more prosperous Venezuela. She wrote with a passion that, given her frail appearance, was surprising. Every single word, every single line, and every single article was a demonstration of their determination and a rallying cry for those who yearned for a change. The media, which were earlier used to spread propaganda for the corrupt administration, became the primary means of communication for the rebels.

In the midst of this cacophonous symphony of defiance, Alejandro and Sofia realized that their roles had been switched. Alejandro, who had in the past protected the status quo, was now coordinating the process that would lead to its demise. In the past, Sofia had participated in the fight for freedom only as a passive observer through her writings; nevertheless, she is now an active participant.

As a result, the foundation for the uprising was laid. As the sun went down on yet another day in Venezuela, the first glimmerings of a new dawn started to appear from the darkness. Both in their own unique ways, Alejandro and Sofia were illuminating the road toward a future that they had the audacity to fantasize about. a future that is free from starvation, persecution, and hopelessness. A possible future in which Venezuela may turn back into the garden of Eden it once was.

Alejandro plotted his strategies, laid out his plans, and made his preparations deep within the vast core of the warehouse. He taught the volunteers, teaching them not only how to handle weapons but also how to harness rage and despair and turn it into a force for change. He did this by teaching them how to channel their emotions.

These followers of his weren't warriors in any sense of the word. They shared the roles of parents, children, and siblings, in addition to being friends. They worked in the fields of baking, teaching, nursing, and auto repair. They were not equipped with uniforms or equipment; the only thing they had was the resolve in their hearts and a common vision of a better world. Alejandro recognized potential in each and every one of them. He watched as the days went by and noticed that they were becoming more than just victims of the catastrophe. They were evolving into the agent that would bring about change.

Alejandro and the other members of his impromptu council of war would spend every night hunched over worn-out maps and discussing possible courses of action. They did an in-depth analysis of the city, pinpointing important places that were essential to their objectives. They continued to argue far into the night, their discussion powered by a powerful brew of black coffee and their iron will. There was no space for failure, especially considering how expensive the price was.

On the other side, Sofia was the movement's beating heart throughout the uprising. Her writings, which were published on flimsy, low-quality paper, ended up becoming their ideology and their rallying cry. She would write in the darkness of the night, the light of a solitary lantern providing the only illumination for her writing. Her hands, which were covered in ink, worked quickly as she attempted to capture the essence of their struggle, their dreams, and their hopes.

She would give her most recent work to the network of runners every morning. The majority of the runners were youngsters because of their youth and quickness, which made them nearly undetectable in the frenzy of the metropolis. They would disseminate these pieces across the city by slipping them under doors, leaving them in public locations, and even having the audacity to hand deliver them to government buildings. The words that Sofia spoke were like seeds, and they were planted in the hearts of people who had the courage to dream of change.

She did not refer to Alejandro by name in her writing, but rather by his actions and the words he spoke. Through her writing, the unknown leader of the uprising was gradually becoming a symbol of hope for a great number of people. People clung to characteristics of him such as his strategic intellect, his strength, and his unshakeable will. These characteristics motivated people and gave them hope.

As Alejandro and Sofia persisted in their efforts, the hitherto inconsequential gang of rebels began to expand. Their cause, which was unknown, became a rumor in the alleyways, a reverberation on the streets, and a well-kept secret among those who were oppressed. The uprising was no longer a pipe dream; rather, it had become a real and expanding force, an impending storm that was building on the horizon of their hopelessness.

The uprising was gaining traction, and the city, which was also their city, was on the verge of a revolution. However, for Alejandro and Sofia, the uprising represented much more than just a struggle for freedom; rather, it was a voyage of self-discovery. A trip that required them to fight against the tide of hopelessness and to cling to the possibility of a better future even when it appeared impossible to do so.

While Alejandro and Sofia were gathering their forces deep below the warehouse's dark depths, the rest of the world was keeping a close eye on Venezuela's political situation. The escalating turmoil was reported outside of the country, which caused the world community to express alarm and engage in speculative thinking about the situation. The writings written by Sofia had become a window into the heart of the uprising, a means for the rest of the world to see and comprehend the fight of the people of Venezuela. These pieces had been translated into a large number of languages.

The echoes of insurrection were motivating people all across the world, not just the people living in Venezuela. Unexpected sources of assistance started to make themselves known and provide their support. Citing Sofia's writings as their inspiration, a non-profit group in Canada launched a fundraising effort to assist the rebels. The rebel organization was able to acquire necessary supplies and, more significantly, obtain access to modern communication technology since cash began to flow into safe accounts in a covert manner.

During this same period of time, the government of Venezuela became increasingly repressive. After the declaration of martial law, all public meetings and curfews were made illegal. Alejandro's techniques needed to be sharper, more elusive. He utilized his experience in the military to devise strategies that would ensure the secrecy of their actions. It was a game of cat and mouse, and the outcome would determine not only their lives but also the destiny of their nation.

In the middle of everything that was going on, Alejandro and Sofia's bond became stronger. They were connected to one another by a shared dream as well as a common adversary, and the presence of the other brought them comfort. The pragmatism with which Alejandro approached problems and the steely will with which he approached them were a source of comfort and a ray of optimism. The reassurance that their struggle had not been in vain was something that he found consolation in thanks to Sofia thanks to her optimistic attitude and fearless character.

They became a safe haven for one another, a place in which they could be honest about their worries, their aspirations, and their desires. Alejandro found himself reminiscing about his time in the military, recounting stories of fallen colleagues and victories against formidable foes. She would listen with her eyes filled with a mixture of admiration and grief, and in return, she would relate stories of her experiences as a journalist, the challenges she faced in her work, and the satisfaction she had when she was able to provide a voice to those who did not have one.

Between these two points in time, the uprising developed into a formidable organization. They were able to persuade more individuals to join their cause thanks to Sofia's words and Alejandro's leadership, and their numbers have been growing steadily over the last several days. Everyone who wanted a better Venezuela found a place for themselves within the uprising, whether they were students, teachers, or shop owners.

However, along with expansion came a number of difficulties. Opinions began to diverge, plans were called into question, and the possibility of a spy in the midst of the group became all too apparent. Both Alejandro and Sofia were forced to contend with tyrants from the outside as well as an adversary from inside their own ranks.

As the days turned into weeks and then months, the uprising began to take on a life of its own. They had evolved from a ragged band of rebels in the beginning into a formidable power that could not be ignored. Their motley crew was gradually developing into a well-oiled machine of resistance, and the warehouse was a hive of activity and buzzing with activity as it did so.

Alejandro worked diligently on the preparation of plans, the formulation of assault strategies, and the coordination of activities with contacts located outside of the city. His experience in the military was extremely beneficial; as a result, he was able to effectively organize, lead, and motivate others. He instructed individuals and organizations in the methods of self-defense, sabotage, and the skill of remaining inconspicuous. In the meantime, Sofia, with her talent for storytelling and her dedication to their cause, provided the outside world with a glimpse from within the uprising as well as a narrative of their battle that was presented in real time.

They started their operation in secret from the shadows. The government supply lines were interrupted, and propaganda posters were replaced with messages of resistance. Additionally, small-scale sabotage operations were carried out. Every seemingly insignificant triumph inspired a fresh surge of optimism and bravery, and their ranks swelled with the passing of each day.

However, along with the growing number of members came disagreement and distrust. Alejandro found himself in the position of having to deal with opposition and suspicions that there was a traitor among them. Some of their members had been apprehended as a result of an impromptu raid that had been conducted on one of their supply sites. During his time in the military, Alejandro had seen enough to know that this was not a coincidence.

He took great care to ensure that neither fear nor paranoia spread throughout their ranks. He was well aware that it would only serve to make them weaker. Together with Sofia, he sought to maintain morale up among the soldiers by constantly reminding them of the reason they were fighting and the Venezuela they were attempting to defend.

At the same time, Sofia's pieces were generating buzz in countries other than their own. The Venezuelan administration was coming under increasing pressure from the international community. Sofia's statements had caused human rights groups, international leaders, and global citizens to take attention of what was going on in the globe. The situation in Venezuela was no longer a remote and foreign issue; rather, it had evolved into a battle for humanity, for freedom, and for justice.

As the strength of the uprising increased, so did the closeness that existed between Sofia and Alejandro. Their connection had developed into something deeper and more intimate; it was no longer only based on the fact that they had similar aspirations and objectives. They discovered that they could rely on each other for support and comfort, and that they had a common vision of a future in which Venezuela would be free and its people would once again be able to dream.

However, despite their growing proximity to one another, they were unable to escape the gloomy cloud that hovered over them. This cloud consisted of the unknown traitor, the ever-present danger of being discovered, and the unrelenting grind of their battle. The stakes, the difficulties, and the depth of the shadows all increased day by day as the situation progressed.

The rebel force, which was led by Alejandro, had been organized into several units with particular functions. There were certain individuals whose primary goal was reconnaissance, or the collection of intelligence regarding government operations and supply routes. Another section was responsible for training new recruits and preparing them for missions of sabotage and disruption. A third group was in charge of directing the logistics of the rebellion, making sure that the insurgents always received the supplies and rations they need. And last but not least, there was Sofia's squad, also known as the communications section.

They served as the voice of the uprising. They prepared brochures outlining the horrors committed by the dictatorship, radio broadcasts encouraging the people to rise up, and movies presenting the actual face of the uprising, which were the hopeless but resolute residents of Venezuela. Sofia's abilities as a journalist were utilized in the creation of these materials.

Every message that Sofia wrote or aired pulled in additional people who supported or sympathized with her cause. Her stories were captivating, and her words had an emotional punch. She gave the uprising a human face and a heart, making it more believable. They were not simply nameless rebels; rather, they were families consisting of dads, mothers, daughters, and sons, each with their own unique history of hardship and everyone with their own individual justification for fighting.

However, as their notoriety increased, so did the risk they put themselves in. The government initiated a harsh crackdown, and the actions of the resistance came under increasing scrutiny as a result. The number of raids increased, and the number of informants expanded. Both paranoia and suspicion were ever-present and persistent companions. Alejandro was under continual pressure to uphold the integrity of the group as he investigated who among them was betraying them.

It was an underlying agreement that Alejandro and Sofia would be the deciding factor in whether or not the uprising would be successful. Their leadership and the connection they shared served as the rebellion's primary sources of cohesion. However, the tension was plain to see. The ever-present threat had caused Alejandro's face to become more haggard, and Sofia's eyes had lost some of their brightness as a result. As the severity of their predicament worsened, they only managed to snag a few fleeting moments of tranquility here and there.

During the course of one night, Alejandro and Sofia discovered that they were the only people in the complex of tunnels that made up the warehouse. The atmosphere was thick with worries that were kept to oneself and a determination that was general.

Sofia mumbled, "I never thought we would be here, leading a rebellion, fighting for our lives," as her fingers traced the patterns of a map that was spread out on the table between them. "I never thought we would be here,"

"Me neither," Alejandro acknowledged, his voice ringing in the silence. "But we are here, and we will do whatever we must to give our people their freedom back."

As their gazes locked across the expansive globe, a solemn agreement was made between them in silence. The battle wasn't finished by any stretch of the imagination, and the path to freedom was strewn with peril. However, they were prepared to confront whatever lied ahead of them, side by side, since they were bonded by a same ideal - that of a free Venezuela.

Alejandro, Sofia, and the other members of the resistance would get together in the central chamber of their covert headquarters, which was only barely illuminated. It was always Alejandro's position that choices should be taken by the group as a whole whenever it was practicable. They deliberated over the next steps while seated in a semicircle within their improvised council room, which consisted of rough-hewn stone walls on all sides.

During those few intervals, you could read the hopelessness and determination written on everyone's face. There was a guy named Manuel, a reformed educator who had lost his patience after one too many occasions of seeing his pupils go hungry. Marta was a nurse who had to stand by and watch patients pass away since there was no medication available. And then there was Ricardo, a young man who had only entered his adolescent years but was already orphaned as a result of the crisis.

Each narrative served as evidence of the magnitude of the

adversity that they had encountered. Nevertheless, there was a special power in their togetherness, and an unwavering determination in their common goal. Every single individual played a vital role in the massive machine that was steadily gaining speed. The uprising was gaining momentum, and along with it, the people's optimism increased.

The importance of Sofia's part as the voice of the uprising cannot be overstated. She produced anonymous bulletins describing the government's corruption and violence using the basic printing equipment that they had managed to rescue. Her tales, which were gritty and based on genuine events, stoked the fires of insurrection that burned deep inside the hearts of the downtrodden masses. It was done under the cover of night, with the flyers being slid into letterboxes, put on bus seats, and shared about in marketplaces.

Due to Alejandro's extensive military experience, the tactical actions were commanded by him. He was responsible for orchestrating their daring attacks on government supply convoys, which resulted in the people receiving much-needed food and medical supplies. Even though they were dangerous, these acts of rebellion had a double function. They reduced the suffering of the civilian population while simultaneously undermining the morale of the military commanded by the government.

However, the results of their acts were as follows. The administration struck back viciously, further consolidating its hold on power. There were strict curfews imposed, meetings in public were outlawed, and the internet was extensively monitored. The state-controlled media was saturated with propaganda that blamed the economic catastrophe on foreign involvement, while any mention of the insurrection was mercilessly wiped away.

In spite of this, the uprising persisted and became more powerful on a daily basis. Every obstacle they faced, every sacrifice they made, served only to strengthen their resolve. In spite of everything that was going on, Alejandro and Sofia's bond became stronger. They became closer to one another as a result of working for the same goal and bearing the same hardship. Their friendship, which was born in the fires of revolution, emerged as a ray of light in the midst of the gloomy uncertainties that permeated each of their hearts.

Alejandro, Sofia, and the rest of the insurgents struggle to come to terms with their ever-more-complicated reality, forcing them to make challenging choices and putting everything on the line in their quest for freedom.

Alejandro and his fellow rebels crept like shadows through the labyrinth of alleyways and twisting streets that characterized the barrios of Caracas. In spite of their somewhat haphazard look, they handled their operations with a degree of meticulous preparation and merciless efficiency. Their clandestine actions started to stir the emotions of those who were being repressed, which inspired whispers of rebellion that grew louder with each passing day.

Alejandro did an excellent job of methodically coordinating their activities. He conceived of means of egress, contingency plans, and escape strategies. It was possible to remember the schematics of government institutions down to the tiniest of details, and their patrol routines could be anticipated and circumvented. He turned the strategies of the repressive government against themselves by converting his military expertise into an instrument of freedom and using it against the dictatorship.

Their operations were fraught with peril, yet each victorious raid pushed their spirit to greater heights. Alejandro took the initiative rather frequently, and his steely countenance sliced through the tension like a sword. To his colleagues, he was a guiding light, the personification of their collective aspiration to be free. His composure in the face of peril and his indomitable attitude in the thick of the upheaval served as their anchor in the midst of the upheaval.

In the meantime, Sofia was busy fighting her own problems. She labored till the wee hours of the night, her hands pounding furiously on the worn-out keyboard of her outdated laptop. In direct contrast to the twisted propaganda spread by the regime, her writings and bulletins were full of the truth and presented an attitude of resistance.

The words of Sofia provided a clear image of the reality that exists in Venezuela, which is a canvas of suffering and resistance, of hopelessness and despair.

Her briefings turned into the beating heart of the uprising, sending out a cadence that was heard all throughout the country. They were duplicated, distributed from person to person, and read in hushed tones in homes and cafés around the country. The readers of Sofia's journalism developed a strong sense of defiance as a result of her reporting. The reality that she revealed destroyed the illusion that the government had built, and it gave the people the confidence to question, doubt, and reject what the government was doing.

The dangers increased in tandem with their growing influence. Alejandro and Sofia were both aware that the consequences of their conduct made them targets. Their names were muttered in shadowy places, and their faces were plastered all over official watchlists. But despite this, they did not retreat. Their determination did not falter in the least. They were aware of the persecution that was being directed at them, and they refused to submit.

Alejandro and Sofia were able to find comfort in one another notwithstanding all of their difficulties. Their chats, which were frequently carried out in the cover of darkness, were broken up by the intermittent sounds of gunshots in the distance and the harsh whispering of the wind. They shared their hopes and worries, their memories and aspirations for the future, and in doing so, they forged an unbreakable relationship that would serve as their source of strength when they faced the challenges that lay ahead.

Once the seeds of disobedience were planted, there was no going back; even if the path ahead was filled with peril, there was no other option. As Alejandro and Sofia made their way through the storm, their friendship grew deeper and became more linked with the future of their country. But would their combined power be sufficient to survive the storm that was almost certain to be on its way?

The days of Alejandro and Sofia were filled to the brim with events. The military expertise that Alejandro had was essential to the organization of their rapidly expanding rebel force. He took it upon himself to shoulder the responsibility of organizing the disorganized collection of discouraged people into a cohesive and well-disciplined unit. He devised arduous training routines, took part in the drafting of the strategy, and kept a cool head when it came to making decisions.

The members of the organization came from a wide variety of backgrounds, ranging from disillusioned veterans to passionate young students, and they each contributed to the cause in their own special manner. Alejandro made sure that their abilities were refined and that they had all they needed to overcome the adversity that they would face in their fight. It was largely due to Alejandro's efforts that they started to feel connected to one another and began working toward a shared goal.

On the other hand, Sofia made progress in her own right in terms of both words and concepts. Her work as a journalist and her participation in the resistance movement were complementary to one another. Her writing was improved by the actual experience she received by participating in the uprising, which gave her sentences a more raw and urgent character. At the same time, the rebel group gained a voice through her writing that was heard by a large number of people outside of their local surroundings.

The articles and reports written by Sofia started making their way around in private. People who were becoming disillusioned with the dictatorship secretly printed, read, and distributed the documents as they spread their disillusionment. Her remarks, which were filled to the brim with the truth of their fight and the core of their resistance, found resonance in the hearts of the regular people. Her writing was more powerful than any weapon, and it planted the idea of dissent in the brains of those who read it.

The imprint left by the insurrection became larger as it progressed. There were rumblings of support coming from unexpected sources for Alejandro and Sofia. Underground networks provided resources, sympathetic officials turned a blind eye, and a few wealthy donors even sent money without revealing their identities. Their efforts were creating ripples, their cause was resonating, and gradually but surely, the foundations of the system began to shake.

However, this expansion was not without its associated dangers. In their efforts to put down the uprising, the troops of the dictatorship became increasingly ruthless and desperate. As the number of raids and crackdowns increased, the insurgents needed to proceed with extreme caution to avoid being discovered. As they guided the uprising through these perilous waters, the strategic brilliance of Alejandro and the journalistic prowess of Sofia were put to the test.

Because of all that went wrong, Alejandro and Sofia's bond became even stronger. Their common ordeal led to the formation of a connection that went beyond the political motivation that initially drew them together. Their relationship was their safe haven, their source of strength in the midst of their struggle, and their guiding light when things were at their worst. The seeds of disobedience were firmly established, and the first shoots of revolt were starting to appear.

In the weeks and months that followed, the expansion of the organization brought about both progress and challenges. The number of dissatisfied residents who joined them rose, but so did the likelihood that they would betray or be infiltrated by other members of the group. Alejandro recalled that during his time in the military, he had learned that the strength of numbers might transform into a vulnerability by exploiting the weak links in the chain.

Challenges in terms of logistics arose in conjunction with the expansion of the organization. They had to set up a dependable supply of food, water, and medical supplies, guarantee that every one of the members had a secure place to sleep, and keep a variety of communication gear in working order. Alejandro did not get much rest while he spent his evenings planning various plans and scenarios. Nevertheless, in spite of the weight he carried, he never revealed any signs of stress to the other people in the group. His expression never changed, and his voice never wavered. The members of the group never lost confidence in him, and their admiration for him continued to develop.

In the meantime, Sofia witnessed an expansion of her function as well. In order to protect both herself and the group, she had begun writing under a pseudonym. This allowed her to keep her real identity apart from the controversial pieces that she was publishing. She was well aware that if anyone found out who she was, they would place a target on her back. She was moving people far beyond the confines of their city with her writing, evoking sympathy, igniting fury, and reawakening a need for reform in the process.

She also began operating an underground radio station, where she aired news of the horrors committed by the state as well as the advancement of the resistance. The radio station, a chirping ray of light amid the gloom, evolved into an additional lifeline for the uprising.

Despite this, the danger continued to grow. Each broadcast and essay that was released was a gauntlet thrown in the face of the administration, and each one was more daring than the one that came before it. Every time Sofia went on live, her pulse raced in her chest because she was afraid that this would be the moment when they would be discovered. However, she clung to Alejandro's confidence in her and used it as a shield to protect herself from her worries.

During this time, the two of them continued to get closer to one another. By any stretch of the imagination, this could hardly be described as a traditional courtship. Their date nights consisted of late-night conversations of strategy, their romantic walks consisted of reconnaissance missions, and the sweet nothings they said to one another were words of consolation when they were facing difficulty. Nevertheless, there remained a profound love that endured despite all of the mayhem that was going on. A connection that had been made in the fires of their conflict, it was sturdy and tenacious, much like the uprising that they were leading at the time.

As the days turned into weeks, and eventually months, the resistance continued to grow. They were seeing the first signs of fruit from the seeds that they had planted. However, they were fully aware that the voyage was by no means at its conclusion.

The insurgency was first tested for its endurance and cohesion when the last days of October gave way to the cold of winter. It turned out that an important food store had been stolen and the guards were found unconscious and battered. Alejandro and Sofia had a sneaking suspicion that the crime wasn't a desperate attempt by the population to get food, but a calculated attempt to weaken the resistance.

Alejandro took over the investigation, using his extensive military experience to piece together the clues left by those responsible for the crime. On the other hand, the revelation led to a terrible realization: there was a traitor among them who was betraying their secrets to the authorities.

A sense of fear overcame the insurgency, and the trust that had been painstakingly built over time began to crumble. Recognizing that fear and mistrust can undermine cohesion, Alejandro gave an impassioned speech to the assembled group. He reaffirmed their commitment to the same goal and stressed the importance of trust, asking them to maintain their confidence in each other.

Meanwhile, Sofia concluded that the best way to respond to this betrayal is to raise the voices of those who are fighting back. She wrote a powerful article about the event that became a call to action to show people that their struggle wasn't in vain. Her article struck a chord with the public, which led to support in the form of staff and resources.

The event also helped strengthen the bond between Alejandro and Sofia. In the difficult days that followed, they found comfort and support for each other. As they worked together through the predicament, their bond grew stronger and the group's collective resilience was the main source of strength for the uprising.

But the problem was by no means solved. Alejandro realized that they had only a limited amount of time to track down the traitor; otherwise, the insurgency would find itself in an even more precarious situation. Although Sofia's statements boosted their resistance, Alejandro was aware that they needed to strengthen their internal barriers to ensure their survival. They faced the problem of maintaining trust while identifying and eliminating disloyalty-a difficult balancing act that required their full attention.

The longer the conflict went on, the more was at stake and the higher the costs became. However, the seeds of revolt they had planted took root and grew stronger despite the challenges they faced. Their determination to work together was tested, but like a tree that can withstand a storm, they didn't waver from their stance.
Tensions were high in the days after the incident. Alejandro was put in charge of the group's defenses, had to conduct his own investigations to identify the mole, and still keep everyone upbeat. His military training had not prepared him for the nuances of leading an uprising, when the battlefield comprised much more than simply gun battles.

Alejandro made sure to conduct the investigation stealthily while yet extensively questioning every insurgent. He didn't want to start a commotion or raise any more suspicions. Sofia's perceptive understanding of the human condition led him to regularly seek her advice and trust in her judgment. It was a watershed moment in their relationship when they were both obliged to put their whole faith in one another.

At the moment, Sofia was facing an issue that was personal to her. Authorities suspected her of being the source of a recent positive essay and were making concerted efforts to track her down. Although she had always taken precautions to hide her actual identity, the regime's sudden interest was a sobering reminder of the dangers to which she was exposed. This threat did not deter her; rather, it strengthened her will to achieve success.

Sofia kept at it, and the result was a regular stream of articles that inspired people all around Venezuela to take action. Her words were moving, and they conjured up images of them fighting as one and of their hopes for the future. She used the rebels' bravery and the more covert betrayal from inside into a teaching moment for the strength of their cause. Her words functioned as a beacon, uniting disparate groups and giving the resistance cause a fresh infusion of vitality.

Without anyone knowing, Alejandro and Sofia had begun covertly recruiting trustworthy individuals to join an inner circle that would act in a council-like manner. Members of this group had shown themselves to be unwavering in their commitment to the cause and resilient in the face of adversity. They were given authority over important aspects of the rebellion and were tasked with maintaining peace and order among the rebels.

As winter set in, Alejandro and Sofia felt the weight of their obligations more keenly than ever before. They found peace in the silence they shared despite the chaos around them. Their growing closeness protected them from the raging seas. There was yet a flicker of optimism despite the imminent danger and the freezing temperature. They were confident that no matter what happened, so long as they stuck together, they would be okay.

The bitter cold at the year's end reflected the unforgiving reality that the rebels were up against. But even when the freezing temperatures threatened to penetrate to the very bones of the resistance, it persisted. Their motivation was pure, and they were unwavering in their mission. Alejandro and Sofia were tending to the rebellious seed that had been sown, and it was blossoming into a mighty tree.

On a frosty morning, Sofia read aloud her newest work to an attentive audience assembled in a hidden spot. Her words rang out in the still air, full of hope, resilience, and defiance against the repressive system. Her comments envisioned a corruption- and cruelty-free Venezuela, one in which everyone had a say and the freedom to go about their lives without concern. They were all committed to achieving this goal. Her oratory combined with Alejandro's strategic forethought and leadership energized the group.

Meanwhile, Alejandro worked diligently behind the scenes to assure the group's safety by organizing activities, procuring resources, and enforcing more stringent security measures. With his unflinching loyalty and determination, he emerged as a leading figure in the uprising. The momentum of the uprising was spurred forward by his knowledge and Sofia's inspiring oratory.

New opportunities and threats emerge with the start of a new year. Despite all of Venezuela's problems, Alejandro and Sofia have lit a spark of optimism in the country's population. The carefully planted seeds of discontent had matured into something more robust and determined. They braced themselves for the oncoming storm, their sights focused on the horizon where a new day in Venezuela was just beginning to break.

CHAPTER 6 "DANCE OF DECEPTION"

Caracas was eerily quiet in the wee hours of the morning when the insurrection began to stir. This was a dangerous ballet that only the courageous would attempt to execute. Each and every one of their actions had been carefully scripted and prepared. After all, this was more than simply a dance; it was a dance of deceit, a performance on which their very lives depended.

With his military experience, Alejandro led the charge in these endeavors. With a stealth born of need, he moved silently through the city streets, blending in with the darkness like a chameleon. He planted listening devices, intercepted messages, and even participated in daring acts of sabotage with the help of a network of spies and sympathizers.

In one mission, Alejandro breached a well-guarded military base. His intended victim was a package of papers said to contain the regime's new repressive policies. With his military training and subtlety, Alejandro managed to get past the guards, his heartbeat a quiet drum reflecting the anxiety coursing through his veins.

While Alejandro performed his risky ballet in the shadows, Sofia did what journalists do best: she reported the news. She concealed knowledge and instructions for the rebels in writings that appeared to be about everyday city life. Even more eyes were on Sofia while she danced, so the risk was still there. With each new item that appeared in print, the strain increased.

An insider in the regime's government reached out to her one evening and offered her the opportunity to provide her side of the story in an interview. Sofia was aware of the potential risk and reward. It was a risky bet, but the potential reward was substantial. She entered the lion's lair with a recorder in her purse and her wits about her, her every word a delicate ballet.

Every procedure, every interaction, was a high-wire act demanding poise and dexterity in the face of danger. Any indiscretion would have been disastrous for both their cause and themselves, so they had to learn the art of deceit. Alejandro and Sofia, however, maintained their passion and determination. With each passing day, the dance became more daring, the risks higher.

They concealed their headquarters in plain sight, in a generic apartment that was tucked among many others in a busy district of Caracas. There, the dancers of this risky ballet convened to discuss their next move as Alejandro directed their efforts. Plans were being discussed in low tones and there was an air of defiance in the air, but it was as quiet as the uprising they were attempting to foment. The focal point of the room was a map of Caracas that had been made by hand and was affixed to the broken wall. The map was covered in colored symbols that only they could decipher.

During the course of one late afternoon, Alejandro was leading a meeting in which they were discussing the next steps of their goal. Their objective was a gathering of the regime that was taking place at a nearby barracks. His words painted a picture of what they would experience as his finger followed the path on the map, stopping at important locations along the way. The objective was to put bugs in the conference room without being discovered, a balancing act that needed impeccable timing, painstaking accuracy, and a healthy dose of good fortune.

"The trick is to blend in," Alejandro replied, his tone stern but unruffled. "The key is to blend in." "Remember that we are not trying to start a fight; rather, we are gathering intelligence," the officer said. "The ability to remain unseen is our most valuable asset."

Every member of the team was responsible for a certain task. Some would operate as distractions, drawing the attention of soldiers away from important areas at crucial times. Someone or something else would have been responsible for planting the bugs. They were all aware that getting caught was not a viable option for them. Insurgents who were caught were subjected to gruesome and public executions by the state in the hopes of discouraging future uprisings.

From Sofia's perspective, she was struggling under the weight of the responsibility of keeping her cover story intact. Every time she published an article or gave an interview with a member of the government, she was walking into a possible landmine. With just one slip of the tongue or a mistaken statement, she may be found out. Despite this, the uprising became more powerful and their intentions became more specific with each piece that was successfully coded.

Her dance was a slow waltz that was full of feints and steps that were taken very carefully. She would divert suspicion with a well-timed complement and steer the topic away from potentially risky ground with a well-thought-out inquiry. And she would never, ever stop listening, her journalistic ear picking up rumors and murmurs that she would later relay to Alejandro and the resistance movement.

Each day was a step forward in the conflict, and each operation was a gamble against the increasingly stranglehold that the government had. The insurrection was gaining ground, and the conspirators' elaborate dance of deceit became even more audacious as it progressed. Alejandro and Sofia led the group with unyielding determination, fully aware that the course they had chosen was a one from which there was no turning back. The dance had to go on, the tension was rising, and there was no avoiding the culmination of the situation. But for the time being, they continued to dance, pinning all of their hopes on the prospect of a new day still to come.

The insurgents gained self-assurance and bravery with each mission that was carried out to victory. They started breaking the rules and inching their way closer and closer to the frontier of discovery. The music was captivating, but the dance was getting riskier to participate in. They were driven on by the desire to achieve independence and the fantasy of seeing Venezuela rise from the ashes.

Alejandro would frequently remain awake well into the night in order to plot out their next move. He was thorough, exacting, and cautious, and he always took into account every conceivable consequence. He was aware of how much a single error could set him back. He was aware of the severity of the regime's retaliation on its opponents. In addition to this, he shouldered the weight of duty, which was represented by the fact that the lives of others rested in his hands.

The office of Alejandro was a jumble of all kinds of documents, including pictures, maps, and reports. In the midst of all of this disorder, he was finally able to see clearly and put the pieces of the complex puzzle that is the regime's operations together. He needed to be able to predict their movements and outthink them at every step. This was his dance, which consisted of a game of chess played on an unstable board.

One evening, Alejandro sat alone in the dark light of his office, his attention fixed on a recent photograph of a regime rally. Alejandro was thinking deeply about the image. During it, a high-ranking official delivered an impassioned speech, his features contorted into a mask of zeal and resolve. As Alejandro focused his attention on the other individual, he narrowed his eyes. Something didn't quite sit right with him, like there was a dissonance that was tugging at his instincts.

While all was going on, Sofia's dance led her deeper and deeper into the heart of the government. She had unparalleled access to the inner workings of the dictatorship because to her press credentials and her charming personality, which was able to pacify even the most skeptical minds. She conducted interviews with government officials, went to rallies, and reported on the outcomes. She was simply another journalist in the eyes of the authorities. On the other hand, behind the surface, Sofia was an essential component of the uprising.

Sofia was well aware that she was engaging in risky behavior. Each article that she published and each inquiry that she posed got her one step closer to discovering the truth. On the other hand, she was prepared to accept the risk. The knowledge that she obtained was priceless and served as a lifeline for the resistance, allowing them to stay one step ahead of the authorities.

Now the dance of the rebels was in full swing, a ballet of bravery and tenacity set against the bleak background of a country in distress. They were audacious in their actions, and their goals were crystal obvious. Despite this, with each new stride they took, the music of the dictatorship became louder, becoming an eerie tune that threatened to drown out their own.

Despite this, they continued to dance. They danced for the freedom of the people, for the hope of Venezuela, and for the Venezuela that may be. There was a lot riding on the outcome, and the dangers were much larger. But there was still a long way to go in the dance. The night had not yet reached its full maturity, and the dancers were prepared for anything that may occur. The seeds of insurrection that Alejandro and Sofia had sowed were beginning to germinate and take root. And as the shadows cast by the dictatorship became longer, the dancers of the resistance stood there, prepared to meet whatever was headed their way.

Alejandro saw a pattern in the operations of the dictatorship despite the fact that they were going about their business in a covert manner. They appeared to be concentrating their efforts on a particular neighborhood in the middle of Caracas and strengthening that neighborhood with a large number of soldiers and pieces of military hardware. A peculiar conduct taking into consideration the regime's already-established dominance over the capital city. Alejandro was intent on finding the solution to the riddle, since there was an issue that needed to be clarified.

They developed a fresh strategy with Sofia's help, working together. It was a gamble, and it was perhaps the most hazardous idea they had come up with up to that point. It would be necessary for Sofia to make arrangements for a press pass to attend one of the future internal meetings of the government by utilizing her connections within the media circle of the regime. Meanwhile, Alejandro and his crew would sneak into the protected territory while the meeting was in progress. The mission had two main goals: first, to acquire useful intelligence, and second, to locate a potential vulnerability in the supposedly impregnable armor of the dictatorship.

The days that followed were anxious, and they passed in a haze of preparation and sleepless nights. While Alejandro and his crew worked tirelessly on their training, going through every aspect of their strategy, Sofia worked her connections, charming and persuading everybody she met along the way. Every action and every step had to be honed to perfection; it was like a ballet that had been designed just for survival.

On the day of the procedure, the atmosphere was charged with excitement and nervousness due to the impending operation. Before going inside the meeting, Sofia flashed Alejandro a stern look while dressed in a business suit and sporting a press badge that was fastened to the lapel of her jacket. As Alejandro followed her through the crowd until she was no longer visible, his heart was thumping furiously in his chest.

While Alejandro and his squad maneuvered into position, Sofia bravely entered the lion's lair with nothing but her wits and her courage to defend herself. They pretended to be employees of a local utility company and started their stealthy penetration of the heavily guarded location while wearing their uniforms. Every movement might have been a mistake, and every breath could have been a clue. It was like dancing on the edge of a razor.

As Sofia was being screened by security inside the conference, she held her breath the entire time. After being given the all clear, she entered the auditorium, which was a hive of activity due to the presence of authorities and members of the press. The atmosphere was thick with excitement, and one could feel the intensity in the room. She found a seat, but her heart was racing as she took in her surroundings.

When Sofia saw the high-ranking figure that she knew from the photos that Alejandro had taken on the stage, she felt a shudder go down her spine. She couldn't get her finger on what it was exactly, but there was something about him that gave out a vibe of both authority and danger. As soon as he started talking, Sofia started taking notes while simultaneously observing the entire room and soaking in all of the information.

Alejandro and his colleagues were making headway outside with their work. They had successfully circumvented the early security procedures and were now well hidden within the guarded area. Every second counted, and every minute brought them one step closer to finding the answer. However, they persisted in their search, being motivated by the need to uncover anything, anything, that may provide them with an advantage.

At the same time that Sofia and Alejandro were engaging in their risky dance, the shadow of the government became even greater. The stakes were larger than they had ever been, and the risk was growing with every passing second. However, each in his own unique manner, they were dedicated to the cause of fighting for a better Venezuela. It was a dance of deceit for them, but it was also a dance of freedom and optimism. They continued to dance in defiance of the impending dangers.

Inside the auditorium, Sofia listened intently to the official's address while simultaneously taking careful notes with her pen as it moved quickly across the pages of the notebook, she was using to record them. Her perceptive eyes picked up on the authorities' subtly exchanging looks with one another, their discreet nods of understanding, and the assured stances they maintained. It was more than simply an internal meeting; it was a show of power that was well planned, and it served as a monument to their dominance over the nation.

Not content to merely take in the information, Sofia was actively processing it and attempting to make sense of the hidden meanings masked by the political language. The leaders discussed "fortifying national stability" and "silencing the whispers of dissent" in their statements. Sofia was aware that the message was intended for the regime's supporters despite the fact that it was disguised as an act of patriotism throughout. Because of the ever-increasing strength of their control over Venezuela, she was aware that the success of this operation was more important than it had ever been.

On the outside, Alejandro's crew was making progress in approaching the core of the guarded region. The stress, as well as the level of risk, grew with each passing minute. They moved quickly but cautiously, their faces disguised by the helmets they wore, and their genuine objectives veiled behind the mask of hardworking individuals they presented to the world. They were so quiet that the armed guards who were monitoring the area did not see them as they came by.

Alejandro was in charge of the group, and you could see his pulse beating rapidly with each step they made. He needed to watch his step and use caution. They risk losing their life with even the slightest of blunders, such as making the wrong choice. He readily accepted the duty of bearing the weight of their lives on his shoulders, and he did so by carrying them. It was a burden, to be sure, but it was also a force that drove us on. In order to ensure their existence and provide freedom to their people, he would take on even greater responsibility than this.

In the meanwhile, Sofia had taken away a lot of useful information from the conference. She gained knowledge of the regime's plans to further oppress the population as well as its measures to combat the rising level of opposition. However, she was also aware of the fractures that existed inside their union. The power battles, the divergent worldviews, and everything else were all there, but they were concealed by guileful grins and resolute handshakes. These shortcomings were chances for them, and Sofia was well aware of the fact that she needed to convey this information to Alejandro.

In spite of the fact that her thoughts were racing, Sofia managed to keep a calm appearance while she expertly navigated her way out of the auditorium as the conference came to a close. Alejandro and his squad had made significant progress and were getting closer to the core of the defended region. They were getting closer and closer to the culmination of the dance of deceit, but they had not yet met their most crucial obstacle.

As Sofia made her way out of the building, she realized that the fate of not only her own life but also the direction the uprising would take was in her hands. On the other hand, Alejandro was on the verge of making a discovery that had the potential to completely alter their plan. Both of them were oblivious of what the other had learned, yet they were in sync with one another in their resiliency and drive.

The dance had not even come close to coming to a finish, and the climax of their performance was still to come. They continued to dance despite their unwavering determination despite the fact that it was a dance fraught with perils and secrets, a dance in which the slightest error might be fatal.

As soon as she was able to retreat inside the confines of her temporary office, Sofia hastily scribbled down the information that she had acquired. Her frantic movements on her battered keyboard were necessary to translate the government's jargon into a language that the average Venezuelan could comprehend. Her articles were the vital source of information for the uprising since they provided insights that were not otherwise available.

Outside of the city, Alejandro and his gang had traveled far enough to reach the center of the territory controlled by the government. The facility, which appeared to be a power plant from the outside, loomed menacingly against the backdrop of the night sky. Fear and excitement made Alejandro's heart race as it raced to keep up with his racing thoughts. He was aware that what they were going to attempt was going to put them in danger, but he also was aware that it was something that had to be done.

Alejandro gave a final nod of affirmation to his crew before leading them into the building he was in charge of. They did not make a sound as they proceeded, the continual hum of the machinery masking the sound of their footfall. As a result of Alejandro's training, his senses were heightened, and he was prepared to respond to any hint of danger.

After traveling back to the city, Sofia completed her piece. While her heart raced in her chest, she took a brief pause before clicking the "send" button on the email. She would be putting into motion, with just one click, a series of events that would shake the system to its very foundations, which would cause it to crumble. She inhaled deeply before pressing the key to the door.

While this was going on, Alejandro and the rest of his crew were making steady headway without encountering any resistance thus far within the power plant. They were finally able to enter the control room, which was a confusing maze of screens and controls. Alejandro moved closer to the primary console as his gloved fingers began to play about on the keys. As he worked his way around firewalls and decrypted codes, his expression was one of intense concentration.

As Alejandro worked, the minutes quickly turned into hours. Outside, his group maintained a careful watch, their nerves tense with the expectation of what was to come. The foundations of an uprising were being laid right in the middle of the regime's daily activities. Their every action was premeditated, and every stride was metered out as they continued the dance of deception.

It was no longer simply a matter of surviving; rather, it was a matter of bringing about change. Through her comments, Sofia was presenting a picture of the harsh realities of their life, which served to invigorate the people of Venezuela. Alejandro was taking a direct and deliberate aim at the very center of the government with his acts. The crescendo of the dance was drawing near, and both Sofia and Alejandro could feel the transition that was about to take place as the sun began to rise.

This part of their life, this Dance of Deception, was determining not just their futures but also the destinies of the country they held so dear to their hearts. Their deeds and decisions caused a domino effect that was gradually developing into a tidal wave, a wave that posed a danger to the tyrannical dictatorship since it threatened to wash it away.

But there was still a long way to go in the dance. Because of their acts, they were now on a treacherous path, one that was laden not just with risk but also with ambiguity and betrayal. They needed to watch their step very carefully since the slightest error may lead to their demise. However, when they danced, they felt a feeling of purpose and optimism fill them up at the same time. Their dance was a demonstration of their energy, their determination, and their everlasting yearning for independence.

Sofia leaned back in her chair as the sun began to rise, her fingers aching from the rapid typing she had been doing and her eyes burning from the glare of the computer. Her most recent paper, which was full of unpleasant realities about the dictatorship and had been distributed to the general populace, was a disquieting read. Each phrase, each remark, was a step forward in the clandestine uprising they were waging.

She relaxed, her eyes moving to the view of the cityscape outside her window as she did so. A golden glow was thrown over the weathered structures by the dawn light that found its way inside. Sofia was well aware that appearances may be deceiving and that the city may appear tranquil or even serene to an uneducated observer. The seeming peace was an illusion; below, there was a simmering sense of discontent and defiance.

At the same time, Alejandro had successfully breached the last of the firewalls and gained access to the essential data. As he started downloading the material, he could feel his heart pounding. This was the end. The fruition of laborious weeks of planning and many efforts to make sacrifices. He was so close to winning that he could practically taste it. But there was still a chance of harm coming their way.

They had to get out of the building and make it back to the base of the rebels without getting hurt. After giving one more check on the console to ensure that the download was finished, Alejandro offered a nod of approval to his companions. It was high time that we get going.

They quickly went back over their previous steps, becoming vigilant to every noise and every shadow as they did so. The mood was tight, and the stakes were greater than they had ever been before. Alejandro's palm was tightly grasping his pistol, and all of his senses were acutely aware of their surroundings. A drop of perspiration ran down his temple.

Back at her secret location, Sofia was hard at work on her next essay, which will concentrate this time on the individuals that make up the insurrection. It was essential to remind the general population of the reasons why they were fighting and what was at risk in this situation. She struggled to escape the feeling of dread that persisted in the back of her mind while she worked. Despite her efforts, she was unable to do so. Her concern extended to Alejandro and the rest of his crew. She could only keep her fingers crossed that they were okay.

In the meantime, Alejandro and his party had nearly completed their escape from the power plant. It was both a comfort and a cause for concern that they had not come across any troops up to this point in their journey. Alejandro couldn't shake the feeling that they were being observed and that they were headed into a trap. He couldn't help but feel that they were being followed. The following few seconds would be critical to determining whether or not they were successful in their quest. They moved with extreme caution in the hopes that they would be able to escape undetected by the people who discovered their breach.

Every move, every choice, and every second played a part in the carefully choreographed performance of deceit. It was a dance that required both bravery and fear, hope and sorrow, and life and death. But despite all that was going on, it was very evident that they were not going to back down. They would battle until the very end, dance until the very end, and hope until the very finish of the game.

Their escape route had been meticulously planned; they had memorized every conceivable obstacle and patrol schedule down to the last detail. It was as if Alejandro and his colleagues were ghosts, for they left no trace. Every room they crossed was a constant reminder of the excesses, the audacity and the disrespect that the dictatorship had for the population.

Their way out led them through an abandoned and rusty service tunnel covered with a layer of dirt and debris. Halfway down, Alejandro noticed the hair on the back of his neck stand up. The echo of a distant footstep was picked up by his ears, even if it was difficult to understand through the hum of the machines. They were accompanied by others.

Immediately, Alejandro sent a signal to his crew to get to safety. While he waited, the only sound that could be heard was the tumultuous beating of his heart. With each passing second, the echo of footsteps became more audible as they drew closer.

When Sofia's phone rang, she was busy writing in her apartment. It was a coded message from Alejandro, saying that they were in a dangerous situation. The message broke Sofia's heart. She was aware that there was little she could do to help them directly, but she could still do what she could to help them. Immediately, she set to work to devise a diversion plan.

While Alejandro's team was busy preparing for the potential danger, Sofia sent out a distress call with a secret message for the rebels scattered throughout the city. She claimed to have seen a member of the regime at a location quite far from the power plant. It was a gamble, but if it succeeded, it would divert the attention of the soldiers and give Alejandro and his group a window of opportunity.

Returning to the power plant, we now heard voices in addition to footsteps. The language was recognizable to Alejandro. It was the secret language of the forces. They were talking about a possible location for the target Sofia had just revealed. Their strategy had worked.

Alejandro and his squad charged out after the immediate danger had been averted and entered the tunnel. As they maneuvered their way through the winding and crowded path, every second counted. Although they were surrounded by the pungent smell of wet earth and iron, they could sense the delicious taste of freedom that lay behind it all. Their goal had been achieved, but the act of deception they were committing was far from over. They were victorious in one of the battles, but the struggle continued.

The rest of the day was a mixture of fear and relief as it went on and on. As night fell, Alejandro and his company had successfully arrived at their home base without incident. Sofia, who had been holding her breath waiting impatiently for their return, was finally able to release all the tension she had been holding in. For the moment, they were safe. The rhythm of defiance would continue to echo through their movements as they danced on. But for the night, they'd sleep. They had played their parts well and were ready for the morning and the difficulties it would bring.

The day of the celebration finally arrived, bringing with it the pressure of expectation that had been building up across the city. The dictatorship, keen to demonstrate its power, had spared no cost in accomplishing this goal. The streets were covered in banners, while loudspeakers broadcasted various pieces of propaganda. Increased numbers of soldiers patrolled the area as part of a blatant and obvious display of power intended to deter any form of opposition.

In her apartment, Sofia got ready for the day that lay ahead of her. She went for an ensemble that was understated but nonetheless appropriate for work and would enable her to blend in with the other journalists there. Before she left, she cast a quick glimpse at her image in the mirror in order to mentally prepare herself for what was to follow. Sofia was aware of the potential consequences, but she also knew the significance of their task. This was her opportunity to have a huge effect and to contribute to the development of the future of her nation.

In another part of town, Alejandro was also getting ready. He pretended to be a maintenance worker by dressing in the appropriate attire and obtaining a phony identity card from one of the group's connections. Even though his heart was racing with anxious energy, he gave himself permission to take a minute to relax by shutting his eyes and taking a few deep breaths. Alejandro was aware of the risks associated with the endeavor, yet he did not waiver in his commitment.

When Sofia arrived, the celebration was already in full swing, with journalists and dignitaries mingling together in a sea of chatter and expectation. She managed to keep her emotions under control and have a professional tone as she worked her way through the crowd. But underneath her seemingly unruffled demeanor was an attentive woman who was studying the crowd for any indications of potential problems and taking mental note of the locations of the guards and exits.

In the meantime, Alejandro arrived at the location undetected, appearing to be simply another employee who got lost in the commotion of the event. As he went around the structure, seeking to get closer to the high-level officials and their covert chats, the steady pounding of his heart provided a rhythmic soundtrack to his quest.

Throughout the course of the day, Sofia and Alejandro gave flawless performances of their roles, with each and every action carefully planned to conceal their genuine motivations. While Alejandro was gathering crucial data on the regime's future plans, Sofia's writing became increasingly critical. Her writings painted an increasingly vivid image of the regime's violence.

They had a better knowledge of the adversary they were up against thanks to every piece of information and discussion they overheard. They were aware of forthcoming crackdowns, new laws aimed to silence dissent, and a system that was much more frightening and deadly than they had imagined it to be.

Alejandro found a suspicious person who was mingling with the rebels late in the evening, which provided the first solid lead towards unmasking the person suspected of being a mole in the organization. The suspect was an inconspicuous person who took care not to attract attention; yet, Alejandro's trained eye noticed a pattern in the suspect's movement and noticed that the individuals they talked with were cause for concern.

The two rebels withdrew as the evening drew to a conclusion; their heads filled with the new knowledge they'd just acquired. They had taken a considerable risk, but it had turned out to be profitable for them. However, with their newfound prosperity came a heightened risk. The operations of the rebel organization would not remain hidden for very long if the regime continued to spiral more into desperation. Alejandro and Sofia were both aware that their charade of deceit was not even close to being finished; in fact, it was just getting started.

Both Alejandro and Sofia were able to make it back to their own houses safely, their thoughts racing with the events that had transpired over the day. Even though it was late, neither of them even considered going to sleep. They decided to focus their efforts on meticulously recording all they had learnt instead.

Alejandro began his job in the cramped quarters with the limited lighting. He pulled out a map of the city and marked the sites that were discussed in the talks that he had overheard, creating a plan for the regime's future activities in the city. He created lines linking different locations, therefore producing a web of activity that illustrated the scope of the regime's authority and the projects that they had planned.

His thoughts immediately went back to the shadowy person he had seen at the event that made him uneasy. Who were these people? Where did they fit in the hierarchy of the regime? The responses to these questions were of the utmost importance. Before the enemy could cause significant harm to their operation, Alejandro was well aware that they needed to locate and eliminate the mole they thought was working for them.

In the meantime, Sofia was also actively engaged in her work. She went back and listened to the discussions she had taped, dissecting the terminology used by the dictatorship as well as the consequences of their goals. Her instinct as a journalist compelled her to go further and uncover the underlying motivations behind the situation. In addition to this, Sofia penned a couple versions of articles, which she then carefully constructed in order to conceal the information that she had obtained. She intended to spread these pieces through her underground network, giving the people an unfiltered picture of the activities taken by the dictatorship.

Both Alejandro and Sofia began to feel as though they were being submerged in a sea of knowledge as the hours passed. They comprehended the magnitude of the challenge that before them. The dictatorship was all-encompassing, all-powerful, and very repressive.

But even in the middle of the hopelessness, a glimmer of light appeared. They were successful in their mission to infiltrate a gathering, during which they collected vital information while evading detection. They were demonstrating that the dictatorship was not impregnable by their actions.

They were both experiencing a rekindled feeling of drive, and this was in spite of the growing danger. When it came to using her words as weapons and the truth to bring down the dictatorship, Sofia was more dedicated than ever before. In addition, Alejandro's determination was bolstered, and his military knowledge proved to be essential when pitted against the organized might of the dictatorship.

In the days that followed, the rebels carried out their covert activities in the same manner as before. The writings written by Sofia began to cause a stir in the underground groups, leading an increasing number of people to question the activities of the dictatorship. The intel provided by Alejandro directed the rebels, assisting them in evading the crackdowns carried out by the dictatorship, and enabling them to begin organizing their countermoves.

Their everyday lives had turned into a complicated ballet of deceit, an ongoing game of cat and mouse with the dictatorship. However, in this game, the stakes were not just any old game; they were matters of life and death, freedom, and subjugation. The obstacles that stood in their way were enormous, but Sofia and Alejandro were well prepared to overcome them. They were conscious of the fact that their defiance and the measures they took were illuminating the way toward a more desirable future.

And so, under the heavy shadow of the oppressive regime, the disparate duo of Alejandro and Sofia, and the growing rebel group they represented, moved like ghosts in the night. Their every step was marked by the threat of discovery, their every breath an avowal of the cause to which they were committed.

With a dangerous combination of wits, courage and cunning, they danced the dance of deception, circumventing the controls of the regime and building the foundation of their rebellion. They carried with them the seeds of change, the promise of a better future, and the weight of their people's hope. Every action was a ballet of risk and reward, a tango of fear and triumph.

This dance wasn't without its dangers. They experienced close calls, clashes with soldiers, and moments when discovery seemed imminent. But despite everything, they persevered and drew strength from their shared vision of a liberated country. They knew their path was fraught with danger, but they also knew they had the power to challenge the status quo.

Alejandro and Sofia felt more intertwined than ever. Their daily lives have become a dance, where every move, every decision affects not only their fate, but the fate of the entire city. The dance continues, the music grows louder, the tension mounts, but regardless of the trials ahead, Alejandro and Sofia remain steadfast in their determination. The curtain falls, but their dance is far from over. The stage is set for the challenges of the future, the coming tests of their will and the next chapter of their rebellion.

The skyline of Caracas is painted with a dawn that is just jaw-dropping. The beginning of the day is the same as all the others; the stress in the air is high, and the expectation of the responsibilities that lie ahead can be physically felt. But this one day would bring with it a storm, one that would break friendships, put loyalties to the test, and push Sofia and Alejandro to their absolute limits.

Alejandro is crouched over a rudimentary map of Caracas in an abandoned warehouse that is now acting as the rebel headquarters on the outskirts of the city. He is planning the next steps that they will take. On the other hand, Sofia is putting the finishing touches on an impassioned editorial that she hopes to secretly disseminate to the general population.

Luis, a youthful and enthusiastic member of their team, rushed through the entryway when he was out of breath. This abruptly broke the calm of their morning ritual and caused a disturbance. His eyes are filled with terror, and his face has lost all of its color. He reports that one of the rebel organization's top-secret supply depots was the target of an unexpected attack by forces loyal to the government. This location is known to only a select few members of the rebel group.

The information comes crashing down like a guillotine. There was not a single survivor. The losses were not only monetary; they were a human blow as well. Friends, comrades, and others who shared their goals and ambitions of a free Venezuela were no longer in their lives. They were all profoundly affected by the incident, but the repercussions of the raid loomed even bigger in their minds. The mystery that won't go away is how the dictatorship knew where to attack in the first place.

The tragic event serves as a sobering reminder to Alejandro of the terrible reality of the direction they have decided to go. He had always been aware that their road was one that was loaded with peril, but the harrowing revelation that they lost one of their own had a profound effect on him. He takes the initiative and rallies the crew, expressing his sorrow but also assuring them that their lost teammates would want them to carry on with the mission.

The news comes as a devastating blow to Sofia. She had a close personal relationship with each of the victims, with whom she had joked and swapped tales. The normally stable pen in her palm is shaking erratically right now. Nevertheless, she is aware that she must make use of this suffering, channel it into her job, and let the people recognize the dictatorship for what it really is.

While they are attempting to deal with the consequences, one concern continues to linger throughout their hideout: was there a betrayer among them? It is a frightening idea, and it poses a danger to the harmony that has been so diligently cultivated between them. Once unshakeable trust is now on the verge of being completely destroyed. They are in danger of losing the links that have held them together, and the cohesive unit that Alejandro and Sofia have worked so hard to create is now experiencing stress.

In spite of their pain and uncertainty, Alejandro and Sofia have no choice but to move through with their plans. Their determination grows stronger, and they become more aware of their goal. They were aware that the stakes were huge, but now it has taken on a more personal significance. This tragedy has only served to further solidify their resolve to see the system brought down. The fight for independence has always been the objective, but today it is now a fight for justice, for their friends who have been killed in battle.

Their emotions are filled with the reverberations of their grief, which fuels their drive to move forward. They are preparing themselves for the challenges that lie ahead while Sofia is writing and Alejandro is planning. Even if their links may be severed and their allegiance may be put to the test, their spirits will not be broken. Even while the way forward is clouded in doubt and plagued with an increased level of peril compared to what they have faced in the past, they are aware that they must go for the sake of their comrades, their country, and Venezuela. The story of their revolt isn't even close to being over, so this part of their life isn't yet finished.

The atmosphere within the rebel group has changed significantly since the incident. The once vibrant and energetic room full of determination and camaraderie now carries the weight of grief and mistrust. The once united group has fragmented and each member eyes the others with a silent question in their eyes: who betrayed us?

In these difficult times, Alejandro enters the scene. As a military man, he's no stranger to loss and betrayal, but the impact of this personal loss is difficult to bear. With each passing day, he delves deeper into the investigation. Strategy and planning cards are replaced by lists and timelines as he desperately tries to piece together the puzzle and find the traitor in their midst.

He also notices the change in Sofia. She has become calmer, her eyes dull, which wasn't the case before. Despite her outward calm, he knows she's been hit hard. But in the midst of her grief, her spirit is unbroken. Her journalistic instincts have prevailed, and she has made it her mission to honor the memory of her lost comrades in her words. Her articles are more passionate, her words more provocative, and the loss gives her writing a new depth.

She begins to publish a series of articles recounting the lives of her fallen comrades and highlighting their dreams and hopes. These articles are secretly circulated among the population, humanizing the loss, glorifying the rebels, and exposing the cruelty of the regime. With each passing day, Sofia's voice becomes the heartbeat of the rebellion, a beacon of hope in the midst of despair.

But the atmosphere of mistrust continues to cast its shadow over the group. Accusations and counter-accusations surface, alliances within the group shift, and tempers heat up. The once tightly knit group, a family forged by a common purpose, now stands on the precipice.

But Alejandro and Sofia refuse to let this incident get them down. They become the pillars that hold the group together. Sofia offers emotional support to her comrades with her words, her empathetic nature, and her quiet resilience. Alejandro, on the other hand, keeps them focused on their goal with his military training and unwavering determination, reminding them that their fight is far from over. His words ring through the gloom: "We fight not only for ourselves, but also for those who cannot. We owe it to them."

As the chapter of their rebellion continues, Alejandro and Sofia find comfort in their shared grief and determination. Their relationship deepens, mutual respect becomes a strong bond, and the spark between them becomes a beacon in these dark times. Without knowing it, they have become the heart and soul of the rebellion, the glue that holds the fragments together. Their leadership in the face of tragedy and despair lays the foundation for what is to come.

With each passing day, the tension increases. The hunt for the traitor, simmering resentment, and the looming threat of the regime form a toxic mix that threatens to implode at any moment. Alejandro and Sofia struggle not only to fight the regime, but also to keep their group together. In the midst of this turmoil, they realize that this fight isn't only a fight for the nation, but also a test of their own bonds. A test in which they cannot fail. Their journey continues, full of challenges, as the shadows of their broken bonds continue to hover over them.

The discovery of an insider's betrayal sends shock waves through the group. Alejandro leads the investigation, focusing on the minute details of the incident. He sifts through communications logs, revisits past missions and cross-examines intelligence sources. His military training and dogged determination serve him well as he plunges headlong into his arduous endeavor, trying to discern patterns and connections that could lead to the mole.

At the same time, Sofia takes a different path. Deep in her grief, she channels her sorrow into a memorial series. In her articles, she remembers the fallen rebels and paints an intimate portrait of their bravery, their hopes, and their sacrifices. The narratives she writes fuel the fire of rebellion, strengthen their resolve, and highlight the tyranny of the regime they're fighting against.

In the midst of their investigative work, the relationship between Alejandro and Sofia continues to develop. Through their shared adversities, they have found comfort in each other. Their frequent meetings, where they initially discuss the progress of the investigation, slowly evolve into moments of shared comfort. Their nightly conversations go beyond the incident, mission, and strategies and reach into the realm of shared dreams, fears, and hopes for a free nation.

But tensions within the group persist. Paranoia gnaws at the bonds that once held them together, sowing the seeds of doubt. Fear of another betrayal lurks in the backs of everyone's minds, keeping them on constant alert. Even the most innocuous behaviors are viewed with suspicion. The palpable tension leads to several heated arguments that threaten the group's cohesion.

In the midst of this turbulent atmosphere, the rebel group takes another blow. The regime tightens its surveillance and introduces new regulations that make it difficult for the rebels to move around unnoticed. They have to rethink their strategies and retreat, which increases the feeling of helplessness within the group.

Despite the growing pressure, Alejandro remains steadfast. He holds on to his conviction that they can track down the traitor and continue their fight. His relentless pursuit of the truth in the face of adversity becomes an inspiration to the group, a beacon of hope in their darkest hours.

In parallel, Sofia's articles make waves among the oppressed masses. They're disseminated in secret, their content whispered softly in the darkness of the night, awakening a sense of unity and purpose among the oppressed population. Despite the group's internal struggles, Sofia's powerful narratives keep the spirit of rebellion alive.

As they make their way through these turbulent times, Alejandro and Sofia find that they're connected through their shared commitment to the cause and the grief they have endured. Their relationship, forged in the crucible of shared adversity, becomes a stable anchor amidst the storm that threatens to tear their group apart.

Yet they're acutely aware that the greatest tests of their rebellion still lie ahead. The future hangs in the balance and is filled with uncertainty. Their journey is far from over and leads them down a dangerous path. Yet amid chaos and despair, Alejandro and Sofia are determined, the unyielding pillars of a rebellion that stands on the precipice. The echoes of their broken bonds and the betrayals they have suffered strengthen their resolve to face the challenges that lie ahead.

As a result of the recently implemented limitations by the dictatorship, the rebels were restricted to moving only inside the bounds of their covert base. Alejandro found himself delving further into the network of communications in an effort to locate any hints that would point them in the direction of the treasonous actor. His eyes combed through every scrap of information that was accessible, while his thoughts worked through many potential leads and results. His days and nights merged into a single continuous cycle.

Within the confines of their stronghold, Alejandro saw that the morale of the crew was beginning to decline. Their previously vivacious features now displayed fatigue and uncertainty, and the enthusiasm that had resonated in their words had been replaced with a muffled anxiety. He was aware that in order to restore their trust, maintain their unity, and remind them of the reasons they had begun the uprising, he needed to do three things.

During this time, Sofia was seeing the tangible despondency that was surrounding their group, and as a result, she came to the conclusion that she would use her experience as a journalist to try to brighten their spirits. She started a series of internal briefings to share stories of resistance from across the world, focusing on the necessity of trust inside the group as well as the strength of togetherness. Her remarks, which she communicated with an authentic sense of passion and conviction, started to kindle a spark of hope throughout the group, which became a beacon of light in the middle of the overwhelming darkness.

The relationship between Alejandro and Sofia became stronger as they struggled to overcome the obstacles that appeared to be insurmountable. They were able to draw strength and comfort from their relationship with one another, which served as a source of solace for them both. They frequently found themselves engrossed in talks that lasted for several hours, during which they not only discussed their current situation but also their aspirations and wishes for a free society, a future that they both envisioned and worked for.

Even while it was a source of comfort, their relationship was not without of difficulties. Their responsibilities frequently came into conflict with one another, their techniques were different, and the joint load they carried took a toll on both of them. However, in one another, they discovered a partner, a confidant who shared their worries and goals, and someone who understood the seriousness of their task and the sacrifices it needed of them. Their connection grew into a delicate dance over the course of their time together, balancing the wordless fondness they felt for one another with the brutal reality of their battle against the dictatorship.

Their doggedness started to rub off on the other members of the gang. The members of the group slowly started to come back together as they told their experiences, listened to one other's accounts of overcoming adversity, and committed themselves to providing steady leadership. They were gradually regaining their sense of solidarity, and their determination was growing stronger. The mutters of apprehension were gradually being replaced by murmurs of determination, and the unease was gradually being replaced by a heightened sense of determination.

Alejandro, Sofia, and the rest of their gang maintained their resolve despite the waves of hardship that were slamming upon them. They had not been rendered helpless by the tragedy they had to endure; rather, it had served as a reminder of what was at stake. The links that had previously appeared to be destroyed were beginning to repair, and their determination was taking root in spite of the difficulties they were experiencing.

Nevertheless, they had a long way to go before reaching their destination. They were still being watched by the dictatorship, which was strengthening its iron grasp, and the shadows of the traitor hovered over them. The groundwork for an uprising had been laid, but it was by no means certain that it would bear fruit. During this conflict, the stakes were higher than they had ever been, their relationships were put to the test, and their determination was pushed to its absolute maximum. But despite the odds, Alejandro and Sofia both possessed a resolute determination that refused to go out, like a light that won't go out in the dark. They were aware that they needed to keep moving forward in order to cultivate the seeds of insurrection that they had planted.

As the hours went into days, the sinister phantom of the betrayer remained a persistent presence throughout the uprising. Both Sofia and Alejandro never wavered in their commitment to the cause they were fighting for, but the group as a whole became more divided as a result of the dread and mistrust that pervaded the atmosphere. Former allies within the group started seeing each other with growing levels of mistrust. Allies turned out to be potential foes, and every behavior was analyzed for a clue that they had betrayed the cause.

Alejandro kept moving forward in spite of all that was going on, laboring ceaselessly with his network of spies and informants. They persisted in their clandestine activities, even though doing so put them in grave danger and exposed them to a high level of risk. They hoped that the information they gathered would be sufficient to unearth the traitor and bring them to justice. Alejandro took part in the risky reconnaissance missions personally, and his previous experience in the military came in handy as he eluded the regime's men and made his way past their strong fortifications.

While Alejandro dealt with the bodily threats, Sofia had to contend with the psychological conflict. The cohesion that she had worked so hard to cultivate was starting to come apart at the seams. The tension that had been building up among the members of the gang threatened to break the up the insurrection. When Sofia understood that their ability to trust one another was crucial to their ability to stay alive, she made it her duty to rebuild that trust among them.

She started by organizing group gatherings, during which participants may share their worries and concerns with one another. These meetings were hard, with heated disputes and nasty accusations flying back and forth between participants. Despite this, Sofia acted as their moderator with dignity and tolerance, ensuring that every member's concerns and uncertainties were taken into account and that their voices were heard.

She also maintained her work as a journalist, recording their struggle and bringing awareness to the cause that they were fighting for. The general public started hearing what Sofia had to say, which sparked a subdued uprising outside of their group. They were given a glimpse of hope and a reminder that their effort had not been in vain as the word of the insurrection spread throughout the land.

The relationship between Sofia and Alejandro was not, however, exempt from the effects of the tension. They found themselves to be at odds with one another more frequently, disagreeing about the best way to proceed. The strategic and military strategy that Alejandro used was in direct opposition to Sofia's empathetic and community-focused perspective. The strain that existed between them increased, putting their relationship to the test.

Nevertheless, despite the fact that they had differences of opinion, their bond remained strong. They were able to see past their differences and develop a profound understanding and regard for one another as a result of the struggle that they had in common. Their connection served as a beacon of light in the darkness, a monument to their mutual hope for a better future, and a sign of perseverance despite the fact that their world was falling apart.

Despite the fact that they were closer to one another on a personal level, their fight was not yet done. The regime's despotism worsened with each passing day, and the threat posed by the unknown traitor became more apparent as time went on. Both Alejandro and Sofia were aware that the road they were about to travel was filled with peril. They were aware that the battle they were fighting was not only for their own lives, but also for the very identity of their nation. And in spite of the difficulties they encountered, they did not let go of their determination; their dedication to their cause remained unshaken; and their spirits were not crushed. Their conflict was in no way resolved.

Alejandro and Sofia were able to put their disputes behind them and reconnect, proving that their connection was stronger than the tensions that threatened to pull them apart. They were bound together by their commitment to fighting for a better future for their people and their common belief in the importance of justice.

In their fight against the dictatorship, the journalistic work done by Sofia and the strategic efforts put forward by Alejandro proved to be invaluable assets. In spite of the fact that they had lost a comrade and that one of them may have been a traitor, the spark of rebellion that had been kindled by their bravery was beginning to take fire. Their ordeal, which was fraught with personal tragedy and self-sacrifice, shone a light of inspiration and encouragement on others who were struggling to survive the regime's oppression.

At the end of the chapter, Sofia took some time to write their adventure in her diary. Her comments served as a monument to their strength, endurance, and solidarity throughout the ordeal. On the other hand, Alejandro spent the evening hours plotting their next action, resolute in his goal to bring the betrayer to justice and deal a devastating blow to the dictatorship.

Their relationships had been put to the test and broken, but through their common adversity, they had discovered a resiliency inside themselves that they were not aware they possessed. Their conflict had not even begun to be resolved; rather, it had only moved into a new stage. Their unyielding will, rather than extinguishing their optimism, served as a source of inspiration for them.

A strong sense of resolve permeated the air as night descended over their hidden center of operations. As they prepared for the fights that were to come, they were aware of the fact that they possessed the ability to alter the future of their nation. The seeds of revolt had been planted, and the flame of revolution continued to burn brightly within their souls, shining a light on the way to freedom.

The moving story of perseverance, sacrifice, and unwavering optimism that was left behind was all that was left behind. A story that would go on to reverberate through the annals of their nation's history, encouraging subsequent generations to fight back against oppression and inequality.

CHAPTER 7 "SHATTERED BONDS"

Everything starts off with a pervasive sense of anxiety that sweeps over the nation. The incisive journalism of Sofia shakes the population' belief in the state, leading to widespread discontent as a result of the exposure of corruption and lies that it brings to light. Every day, new exposés make their way onto the airwaves, taking the mask off the fraudulent promises made by the dictatorship and exposing the meaningless words they have to say.

The combination of Sofia's writings, the audios, and the films causes shockwaves of outrage and incredulity among the population of the city. The population, which used to live in dread and uncertainty, now openly questions the government that has been in place for so long. Quotes from Sofia's writings, caricatures of corrupt officials, and slogans of resistance start to appear as graffiti on the walls of the city. Revolution begins as whispers, then becomes murmurs, and then becomes loud shouts.

In the meantime, Alejandro, well aware of the gathering steam, seizes the opportunity presented by the upheaval. He has a history in the military, and he is leading the rebels in a series of daring moves that are aimed at disrupting the operations of the state. They break into government warehouses where food and medical supplies are stored, redistributing the limited resources to the disadvantaged community in order to garner even more sympathy for their cause from the general populace.

Their self-assurance increases with every assignment that is completed successfully. There is an increase in the number of people eager to aid the rebels by either giving them with information, refuge, or joining their ranks. The number of rebels and their overall impact both continue to increase. The efforts of the authorities to discredit and silence them appear to just add gasoline to the already-smoldering spark of insurrection.

However, the increased danger that they are taking comes hand in hand with their growing bravado. The dictatorship is driven to desperation, at which point it retaliates with ruthless force. In certain regions, a state of martial rule has been declared, and as a result, arrests have been made and curfews have been imposed. This repressive response does nothing more than legitimize Sofia's exposés and enhances the will of the population to oppose the dictatorship.

At the center of it all, Alejandro and Sofia continue to grow closer to one another. Their bond grows stronger, not only as allies, but also as two individuals who have made the conscious decision to go against the grain together. In spite of the insanity that is occurring all around them, they are able to find moments of calm and comfort in one another's presence. While Alejandro organizes the next moves for their resistance, Sofia continues her profession as a journalist. The trust that they have in one another is their most important and valuable asset.

They are still haunted by the events that occurred in the past, but much like a phoenix that rises from the ashes of its fallen home, they are moving on with their lives and utilizing the anguish and sorrow that they have endured as fuel for their struggle. Every expose and every successful operation are a monument to their resiliency, an homage to their departed companions, and a step closer to the justice that they so desperately desire.

As daring acts of revolt against a repressive dictatorship start to disrupt the political landscape, the public watches transfixed as these events begin to bring about change. In the middle of their people's struggles, Sofia and Alejandro have lit a light of hope for their community, which is at the center of a revolution that is currently in the process of developing.

Every piece that she writes is like a spark, igniting the simmering tension within the public and turning the simple murmurs of dissatisfaction into loud, resonating pleas for change. Her writing is like a spark because it is like a spark.

Shockwaves are sent out throughout the city as a result of every piece of evidence that she brings to light and every corrupt conduct that she exposes. The evil that was formerly concealed in darkness has just been brought into the glaring light of the truth. Armed with the understanding of the regime's actual character, the populace starts to perceive the figures of power not as defenders but as oppressors.

Alejandro, ever the strategist, takes advantage of this interruption by using it to their advantage. Using his previous service in the military as a resource, he concocts audacious and risky plans to exploit the regime's vulnerabilities. The insurgents are acting with a newly discovered assurance, and their actions are becoming both more daring and more regular. They carry out daring attacks on military convoys, demolish surveillance equipment, and disrupt the regime's communications while at the same time assisting the most defenseless members of the population.

Alejandro and Sofia's bond continues to strengthen. Their original connection, which was formed in the fire of a common sorrow, becomes even stronger as they labor assiduously side by side for the advancement of their cause. Alejandro, who led with a level head and military precision, and Sofia, who was the voice of the uprising, her words serving as a rallying cry to the people of the city to fight against the corrupt government. They find comfort in one another's companionship in the early hours of the morning, when the rest of the world is still asleep, and take strength from their common vision of a better future.

However, there is a correlation between increasing success and increased danger. As the dictatorship becomes aware of the growing danger, it responds by imposing more regulations and putting on a more violent display of power. A curfew is ordered to be implemented, individuals' freedoms are curtailed, and heavily armed troops begin patrolling the streets. However, now that they are aware of the actual character of the system, the people refuse to be quiet. People all around the city begin publicly questioning and contesting the authority of the dictatorship by staging spontaneous demonstrations.

Alejandro and Sofia never lose sight of the cost of their revolt despite the fact that the opposition is growing more intense. They keep the memories of their slain colleagues close to their hearts as a constant reminder of the high price that they may have to pay themselves. The hope that one day they will live in a society that is both free and just gives them the strength to rise from the ashes of despair and take on whatever challenges life throws at them.

The uprising is reaching a crescendo that has not been seen before, and the reverberations of their defiance can be heard in every nook and cranny of the metropolis. Their battle is far from finished, but the seeds of hope have been planted, and they watch them bloom, nurtured by the unshakable courage and tenacity with which they have fought up to this point.

The rebels, who are being commanded by Alejandro, are keeping up their audacious operations against the dictatorship as they continue their dogged pursuit of their cause. Each and every evening is a tango with peril, a game of shadows played out beneath the cover of the curfew. Every piece of graffiti scribbled on a city wall becomes a possible signal for the next attack, while the city's secluded nooks and crannies are transformed into their clandestine gathering places and lookouts.

They devise a complicated system of codes and indicators that are undecipherable to those with untrained eyes but serve as a compass for every member of the resistance movement. A wayward bit of chalk makes a mark on a lamppost, which serves as a signal for a hidden cache of supplies; an apparently random series of garbage cans that have been knocked over serves as a guide to a safe house.

Alejandro demonstrates that he is a formidable opponent in this covert game of chess. Every action is analyzed, and every choice is contemplated in light of the possible consequences. However, in spite of the perilous terrain they travel, he takes precautions to ensure that no one working under his direction is unduly endangered. His approach to leadership is characterized by a harmony between military discipline and sympathetic understanding; it is this equilibrium that inspires trust and respect among the insurgents.

In turn, Sofia continues her job as the voice of the uprising in this role. Her reports, which are now being passed about in the shadows and only being read in hushed tones, stoke the fires of dissent among the populace. Her remarks are an energizing combination of cold, hard facts, humorous tales from her own life, and an impassioned call to action. They give a clear picture of the corrupt nature of the dictatorship, of the courageous deeds taken by the rebels, and of a hope for a brighter tomorrow.

The personal danger that Sofia and Alejandro are in is growing in tandem with the escalating stress. The dictatorship is starting to understand the significance of Sofia's words, as well as the tactical genius that lies behind the activities of the rebels. Their identities are spoken in murmured talks within the ranks of the military, and the regime's informants have drawn sketches of their features.

They continue on defiantly in the face of increasing peril, despite the fact that the dictatorship is tightening its hold. The demonstrators are emboldened as a result of the words said by Sofia and the deeds carried out by the insurgents. They are standing their ground in the face of the armed troops, chanting to break the stillness of the night and brandishing the homemade placards they have constructed as if they were shields. The more that the dictatorship tries to put out the flames of dissent and insurrection, the more intensely those flames will burn.

As they continue to engage in this risky dance together, Alejandro and Sofia realize that they are becoming closer to one another. Their common adversity helps to forge a close relationship between them, one that goes beyond the immediate confusion and unpredictability that surrounds them. They not only discover a partner in revolt in one another, but also a light of hope and a source of consolation in one another. Their common goals, the challenges they face together, and the decisions they make together all contribute to the solidification of a partnership that was forged in the fire of a common purpose.

Each new day presents them with new problems, but it also serves to fortify their determination. They make up for every stride they take back by taking two leaps forward. And much like the legendary phoenix, they keep on rising, undeterred, unbroken, and unstoppable in their progress.

One day, the rebel organization eventually achieves their goal of effectively infiltrating the regime's bureaucracy by carrying out a series of covert operations. A low-level employee who is sympathetic to their cause starts passing them crucial papers to utilize in their campaign. These documents have information that is extremely damaging, and it is contained inside them. While Alejandro is able to understand coded military communications thanks to his knowledge in the military, Sofia utilizes her investigative skills honed as a journalist to unearth the trails of corruption and illegal power agreements.

Once the material has been analyzed and validated, it will serve as the foundation for some of Sofia's most powerful writings to date. The records provide evidence of a corrupt network that is deeply ingrained in the functioning of the dictatorship. The meticulously prepared pieces written by Sofia shed light on corrupt practices carried out by the government, including the theft of public funds, the illegal sale of weapons, and the enrichment of the governing class at the cost of the average populace.

In spite of the government's frantic efforts to stifle the spread of the news across the city, it quickly becomes widespread. The printing of Sofia's words is done in secret, and they are sent around during the night by hand from door to door. As a result, the items become the deadliest illegal goods in the city. Citizens who are terrified but also more confident are reading the news and discussing it in hushed whispers as their eyes are opened to the extent to which the dictatorship has betrayed them.

The city, which used to be submissive and fearful, is now tense with dissatisfaction and rage. Once a rather uncommon occurrence, protests have evolved into a regular part of daily life. What was once the effort of a very tiny insurgent group has already prompted a profound change in the ambiance of the city. Alejandro is able to detect a gradual transformation in the atmosphere, one in which hopelessness is giving way to defiance and fear is giving way to a fearful rage that is building.

In the meanwhile, Alejandro's predictions about how the dictatorship would respond came true. They become more vicious and desperate as time goes on. The number of soldiers stationed in the city rises, and the curfews that are in place are strictly enforced. The frequency of the raids increases, and the populace are left living in constant terror of being sucked into the jail mills run by the authorities.

Despite this, the masses' resolve only grows stronger as the regime's repression becomes more severe. Each and every instance of violence, each and every wrongful arrest, and each and every falsehood that is exposed simply serves to stoke the fires of insurrection. The reports that Sofia compiles ensure that this is the case. The obvious and unmasked corrupt behavior of the regime is currently receiving a lot of attention. The people and the regime both sense that a shift is on the horizon and are preparing for it accordingly.

In spite of the triumphs, the actions of the rebel organization are becoming increasingly dangerous. The more they engage in illegal activity, the greater the likelihood that they will be found out. Alejandro beefs up their security, guaranteeing that their covert operations will continue to operate undetected by the authorities. The rebel squad is able to stay successful, focused, and secure thanks in large part to Alejandro's extensive military skill, which adapts along with the shifting circumstances that they face.

In the middle of everything going on, Alejandro and Sofia's connection grows stronger. They find solace in one other's silences, strength in each other's determinations, and hope in each other's aspirations. They are not just opponents of the current government; rather, they are allies who support and rely on one another at the most trying of times.

It is now abundantly clear that the unrest has spread beyond the boundaries of the city. After having been disseminated originally exclusively within the bounds of their city, the pieces written by Sofia have now made their way to neighboring regions, sparking rumblings of discontent and dissent in locations that were formerly the regime's strongholds. The narrative of the country is beginning to shift as the realities that were previously hidden by the regime's iron hand become more widely known. The cruelty and corruption of the dictatorship, which were once only rumors circulating in the shadows, are now becoming ever more public knowledge.

The insurrection keeps up its careful balancing act with peril, and its members continue to go through each day fully aware of the possibility that it will be their last. Even though it has been shaken, the dictatorship still has control of the country's military, its police force, and the essential infrastructure of the country. The rebels are well aware that in order to prevail in this conflict, they will have to chip away at the power structures of the regime and eventually bring them down piece by piece.

Every single activity that is carried out by the insurrection needs meticulous preparation and flawless execution. Alejandro seldom gets any sleep since he is so busy painstakingly planning their next move on a map that is laid out on the table in their improvised operation center. The weight of this duty, which rests squarely on his shoulders, is made apparent by the fact that each choice he makes may determine the fate of his comrades in the resistance.

Sofia is unwavering in her commitment to take part in these perilous operations, despite the fact that she has recently become known as the voice of the revolt. She is of the opinion that the fact that she is a journalist does not absolve her from the necessity of taking risks. She fights against the dictatorship by deftly using her pen, but she also conceals a weapon on her person in case things get even more dangerous. She is just as committed as Alejandro is to making sure that their mission is successful, and she refuses to sit on the sidelines.

The fact that they both have a strong sense of duty and drive only serves to strengthen their connection. Alejandro and Sofia frequently find themselves to be the only ones up late into the night, and they spend this time contemplating their next move. They talk ideas, fight about techniques, and sometimes just sit in quiet to share their worries and hopes while doing so. All of this takes place over hot mugs of black coffee. Despite the fact that these moments of connection were borne out of need and a common struggle, they have a tremendous effect on both of them, bolstering their determination and bringing their partnership to a new level of stability.

However, as a result of the increased actions of the rebellion and the desperate efforts taken by the dictatorship to retain control, the tension within the city reaches a point where it begins to boil. The streets are teeming with heavily armed troops, and the presence of their foreboding presence spreads lengthy shadows over the landscape of the city. It is a stifling environment, one that hints at the possibility of a dramatic explosion in the event that the pressure continues to build up.

In spite of the enormous dangers and obstacles, Alejandro and Sofia have not been shaken from their determination. The possibility of harm simply serves to strengthen their determination. There is no going back now since the Phoenix has risen from the ashes. Their struggle for independence, despite the fact that it is plagued with risk and sacrifice, is one that they freely engage in. They do so equip with bravery, resiliency, and an unwavering confidence in the justness of their cause.

As the days progress into weeks, the insurgent group's ability to carry out covert operations improves along with it. In order to teach the members of the organization, Alejandro draws on his experience in the military. As a result, the formerly disorganized gang of freedom fighters quickly transforms into a strong resistance force.

Building a shelter network around the city is high on Alejandro's list of priorities as he works to stabilize the situation. These safe havens provide the insurgents with a place to congregate, communicate with one another, and get some much-needed rest. They also stockpile essentials for dealing with unexpected events, such as food, water, and medical supplies. There are even those that provide Sofia with printing presses for her publications.

For her part, Sofia is dogged in her pursuit of various journalistic opportunities. Her pieces, which have since been translated into a variety of languages, have started to travel throughout the globe. This raises awareness all around the world of the corrupt nature of the regime as well as the developing dissatisfaction in their country. The situation is starting to get attention throughout the globe, which will likely result in increased international pressure on the government.

However, the triumph of the uprising will not come without a cost to those involved. Every success, every scandal that is brought to light, and every act of disobedience is greeted with escalating brutality on the part of the regime. Citizens who are suspected of having sympathies with the rebels are subjected to frequent harassment, including having their houses searched and having their belongings taken away. The regime's strategies are becoming increasingly desperate, and its deeds are becoming more horrible.

In the middle of this severe repression, Sofia learns that a large number of people have been detained in one of the city's most impoverished neighborhoods. This neighborhood is well-known for its outspoken opposition to the dictatorship. The news had a profound impact on Sofia. She is well aware that these neighborhoods, which were already struggling under the weight of poverty and neglect, are now receiving the brunt of the regime's fury as a direct result of their courageous activity.

Both Alejandro and Sofia are in need of making a difficult choice. They have two options: either they can carry with their activities as planned, or they may redirect resources to assist the persons who have been detained and their families. They are all in agreement, despite the fact that the decision is challenging, that the uprising ought to be about the people. They are unable to turn a blind eye to the misery that is being inflicted on the very population whose freedom they seek to secure.

As a result, they go on a dangerous rescue mission. They were able to release numerous prisoners from a makeshift jail by utilizing the information collected by their sources working within the regime. The facility was only partially secured. They are taking a significant risk, but if they are successful, it will boost the spirit of the insurrection as a whole and garner them even more respect among the populace.

The insurgents are no longer operating clandestinely; rather, they have come out into the open and are directly confronting the regime. The regime, in the meantime, is seeing its power dwindle as the persistent efforts of the rebels fracture the veneer of control that it has maintained. Their hard-won gains are put in a gloomy light by the impending specter of the regime's vengeance, which is happening at the same time as the Phoenix is rising. It is a dance on the razor's edge, a delicate balance that must be maintained. The entire cost of their intransigence won't become clear until much later.

After the rescue operation was completed without incident, Alejandro and Sofia have a better understanding of their respective roles in the uprising. Alejandro, using his strategic intelligence, begins coordinating with other movements around the country that are analogous to theirs in the hopes of establishing a unified front. It is becoming more widely known that he is the head of the insurrection, as well as a skilled strategist who is unfazed by the immense weight of the duty that he bears.

On the other side, Sofia discovers that her voice is increasingly becoming the lone guiding light toward the truth in a society that is being suffocated by falsehoods and propaganda. She gives her full attention to her writing in addition to volunteering in the neighborhood. She not only publishes in-depth articles describing the corruption of the dictatorship and the development of the uprising, but she also writes cheerful and inspiring articles that seek to motivate the oppressed public and keep their spirits high in these tough times.

As more and more foreign news sites take up Sofia's stories, the entire globe waits with bated breath. Her evocative accounts of life under the dictatorship and the tenacity of the revolt reach an international audience and influence how people across the world view their fight. When the residents perceive that their battles and resistance are being acknowledged on a global platform, it instills in them a sense of pride and gives them a fresh sense of hope. The essays written by Sofia serve as a tribute to the bravery of the group as a whole and the power of their collective spirit.

The regime's influence is beginning to wane as a result of the escalating dissatisfaction and resistance that is taking place. It becomes clear when a senior individual inside the administration, Minister Alvarez, betrays their cause and turns against them. Alvarez, who was formerly a devoted servant of the government, had been disillusioned after seeing the level of cruelty and corruption that the leadership was ready to commit in order to keep their hold on power.

He approaches the insurgency in a stealthy manner and offers intelligence in exchange for security. Alejandro and Sofia make the decision to meet him despite their reservations because they see the potential benefits of the encounter. At a covert gathering, Alvarez turns over a cache of documents, including evidence of the regime's corruption, their plans to put down the uprising, and, most importantly, the sites of underground jails where dissidents are being imprisoned.

The information about Alvarez's betrayal quickly travels across the rebel group like wildfire. It is a significant triumph because not only do they now have access to important intelligence, but the sheer fact that a high-ranking official has defected from the dictatorship indicates that it is losing control over its subjects. On the other hand, they are aware that the regime will be in a desperate state and pose a greater threat than ever before.

As the rebels' pore over the documents and the information provided by the detainees, they come to the realization that the work that lies before of them is enormous. his determination is strengthened by the knowledge that they are now closer to the heart of the regime than they have ever been before. Alejandro, Sofia, and his fellow rebels prepare themselves for the conflicts that are to come. After it has been reborn, the Phoenix is getting ready to fly straight into the midst of the raging flames.

As the rebels process the information that Alvarez has given them, they start formulating their strategies for the next move they will make. Alejandro and his strategic team are putting in a lot of hard effort to coordinate many simultaneous strikes. They are leveraging the information they have obtained about the regime's military might as well as the hidden places. This would serve two purposes: it would be a rescue operation for the political prisoners, and it would be a display of power by the rebels, sending a clear signal to the regime that they were a force that needed to be taken seriously.

However, the success of the strategy is contingent on its implementation staying a secret, as a leak would result in the inevitable passing of many people. Only those individuals who are actively involved in the activities are made aware of the specifics, as the leadership takes precautions to assure this. They split the overall plan down into smaller pieces, with each team understanding only their unique function and having no knowledge of the bigger vision.

During the time when Alejandro and his crew are getting ready for the next operations, Sofia will be taking on a new but no less essential duty. She writes a series of articles to shed light on the corrupt practices of the administration, using the information she gleaned from Alvarez's betrayal as well as the records they now held. Because timing is crucial, the articles needed to be released in sync with the planned actions of the uprising in order to have the most possible impact and give the population hope.

As Sofia starts to write, her hands shake because the pressure of the work is putting a lot of strain on her shoulders. She is well aware that the words she writes have the potential to stoke the flames of rebellion in the hearts of everyone who takes the time to read them. As a result, she gives everything she has to the job since she feels a strong sense of obligation for the individuals she serves.

The uprising is working with increased strength, and as a result, there are changes occurring in the inhabitants' day-to-day lives. The oppressed people receive Sofia's writings as well as rumors of the rebellion's daring rescue operations, both of which plant the seeds for hope and the guts to act on those hopes. This hope is tangible; it can be seen in the employees' straightened backs, heard in the melodies that youngsters sing in the streets, and seen in the bold graffiti art that begins to appear on the walls of the city as a monument to the spirit of revolt.

On the other hand, when the dictatorship becomes aware of the growing tide of resistance, it responds by increasing its level of repression. The military presence in the cities increases, and curfews are carried out in a very harsh manner. The propaganda machine that the dictatorship uses works around the clock to spread signals that the regime is strong and stable. However, the general public is able to see through these feeble attempts. The dictatorship formerly had an air of invincibility, but it is beginning to lose that aura, and the populace can feel that the tide is moving against them.

Alejandro and Sofia are able to find comfort and support in one another amongst all of these challenging circumstances. Their connection grows stronger not just because to the fact that they have similar beliefs, but also due to the fact that they have similar experiences in leading a revolt and in sharing the hopes and concerns of their people. They grow to be seen as the epitome of the uprising, particularly Alejandro as the unwavering commander and Sofia as the forceful voice. They maintain their solidarity and are prepared to confront any challenge that may be thrown their way.

CHAPTER 8 "THE PHOENIX RISES"

The day that will decide everything arrives with the typical chilly morning air, and the city goes about its business as if nothing is happening. In the early hours before morning, Alejandro, Sofia, and the other members of the rebel group get together for the very final time. The final plans are discussed, possible issues are analyzed, and any necessary adjustments are made at the very last minute. Reiterating his confidence in his companions and the justness of their cause, Alejandro maintains his steely composure throughout the conversation. Sofia, using words that are just as fierce as her energy, helps to rally the group's spirits. Both leaders have given their word that they would do all it takes to protect the members of the organization and maintain the smooth running of the activities.

Every person who was involved in the plan walks away from the meeting with a more resolute intention, the burden of their responsibilities being heavy but not insurmountable. Sofia chooses to remain behind and waits for a signal from Alejandro before she hits the 'publish' button on her expose. She gives her piece, which is a stinging indictment of the dictatorship, one more glance before waiting for the appropriate moment to publish it.

While all is going on, Alejandro, in the appearance of a common laborer, is blending in with the early morning population in the city. He exudes an air of serene composure, which is in stark contrast to the roaring tempest of expectation that is going on inside of him. He gives himself some reassurance by telling himself that this is the moment they have been working toward, the time when all of their sacrifices will pay off.

The predetermined actions start on the edges of the city when the city limits begin. According to the information that they have, the troops of the government are dispersed, and their emphasis is being concentrated on preserving public order. The striking squads of the rebels take advantage of this temporary breakdown in security and slip through the holes without being discovered.

The first things to be taken out are the communication networks.

The unique expertise that Alejandro possesses in military strategy and strategy in general. They do it with lightning speed, crippling the primary communication channels used by the military. This temporarily renders the government unable to see or speak, which throws their response into complete disarray. The first step of the plan is carried out successfully, and Sofia is the one to receive the signal from Alejandro.

The unusual lack of activity on the regime's channels, which are normally very busy, has the city's residents perplexed. When word starts to get around about Sofia's piece, they go from being confused to being shocked. One by one, they peeled back the layers of deception that the administration had created. The brutality and the corruption were right in front of their eyes the whole time. It seems as though the news is going about like wildfire, being transferred from person to person and home to house, and it is lighting the city on fire with its discoveries.

The regime is taken aback by the development. The unexpected shutdown of their communication routes, in conjunction with the revelation that has been made public, sets the ideal conditions for a perfect storm of pandemonium. They are scurrying to respond, but the harm has already been done. The disclosures start to educate and infuriate the people, who then begin to rebel against the government. The formerly subdued masses have now transformed into swarms of demonstrators, and their yells can be heard throughout the streets.

While everything is going on, the rebels is taking advantage of the confusion. The second stage of their strategy is put into motion while the government is preoccupied with other matters. In order to free their comrades, groups of insurgents have infiltrated the prison institutions where they are being detained. Already understaffed as a result of the rising discontent, the security personnel are unable to keep up. The convicts are let free, and the rumors that circulate about their release give fuel to the gathering fire of insurrection among the populace.

On the other hand, the dangers increase with every passing second. Alejandro is aware that they are running out of time. The troops loyal to the government are in the process of reforming, but their window of opportunity is quickly shrinking. Before they are completely overpowered, the rebels have to carry out the last step of their strategy and then retreat.

Nevertheless, despite all of the mayhem, there has been a change. The city, which was once a symbol of hopelessness, throbs with optimism at this very moment. The inhabitants have learned that they are not powerless as a result of the daring activities taken by the uprising. The words of Sofia and the leadership of Alejandro have sown the seeds of revolt, and now those seeds are beginning to sprout. The phoenix, which had been buried beneath the ashes of oppression, is now beginning to rise.

The intensity of the mayhem increases as the brilliant afternoon light beams brightly over the metropolis. The people have taken to the streets, raising their collective voices in a resounding call for freedom and justice. They take to the streets, carrying banners, shouting slogans, and their eyes are blazing with a newly discovered determination. The dictatorship is losing its hold on the city, and the tangible terror that is spreading among their ranks is a direct result of this.

From the cover of their hidden stronghold, Sofia watches the events unfold with an unusual mix of dread and pride. She watches as her words become the rallying cry for those who are oppressed, and she watches as the city that she loves starts to throw off its restraints. However, she is aware that this is only the beginning of things. The government will put up a fight, and when they do, the repercussions might be catastrophic.

In the meantime, Alejandro is deep into the region controlled by the enemy. He and his squad were able to sneak inside one of the regime's most important outposts with the intention of rendering it powerless. They move as stealthily as possible, removing potential dangers and disabling pieces of equipment while using the information they've obtained. They are aware that their window of opportunity is closing quickly, and the dictatorship is putting its soldiers on high alert in preparation to put down the uprising.

However, the rebels have a strategy in place. When Sofia returns to the base, she immediately begins spreading false information. She does this by spreading fake rumors of assaults in various regions using the communication routes that have been broken by the regime. The goal is to disperse the regime's forces as much as possible so that Alejandro and his crew have enough time to finish their job.

It is effective. The armed forces of the dictatorship are dispersed around the city in an attempt to deal with supposed dangers that do not exist. The objective of Alejandro's squad, which involved laying explosives across the outpost, is successfully finished. They get it out of there in the nick of time, as the outpost bursts into flames only seconds after they have finished clearing the perimeter.

The rebels are inspired to begin their uprising when they see the outpost in flames. It is evidence that the regime is not impregnable and that they are susceptible to being overthrown. As the news makes its way across the city, it sparks a new round of demonstrations. The will of the people is not broken but rather fortified by what is happening. The message sent forth by the rebels is unmistakable: they will not retreat.

Alejandro and Sofia get a little moment of calm together among all of the mayhem. Both of them are worn out, and the weight of their respective obligations is weighing heavily on their thoughts. However, there is a flicker in their eyes that indicates a mutual comprehension. This is only the beginning of things to come. Their conflict is in no way resolved. However, for the first time in a considerable amount of time, there is cause for hope. The phoenix has arisen, and its rebirth will not be put down without a fight.

When evening arrived in the city, it created deep shadows across the streets, which were now completely vacant. The inhabitants, exhausted from the demonstrations and tumult that had occurred during the day, had returned to their homes with the screams for justice still ringing in their ears.

After returning to the base of the rebels, the squad reorganized themselves. In spite of the fact that they were exhausted, the members were overjoyed since they had just achieved a huge win for the first time. Their meticulous preparation had been successful. They had succeeded in bringing the regime's corrupt practices to light and dealt a severe blow to its authority. Their deeds had triggered a chain reaction of occurrences, which in turn had motivated the populace to take action.

Alejandro, in spite of the exhaustion that was pulling him down, was right in the thick of things. He was organizing the movement of rebel teams around the city and making sure that everyone was safe and accounted for as they moved from one location to another. Because of his expertise in the military, he has the abilities necessary to effectively plot and manage the rebel organization, and it was only natural that they would unite behind him.

On the other hand, Sofia was preoccupied with her own responsibilities and activities. Her essays and exposes on the dictatorship were widely disseminated across the city, which stoked the flames of revolt and stoked the turmoil that it caused. Now that she had the upper hand, her main priority was to keep the momentum going. She continued to circulate her stories, using her pen as a weapon against the repressive dictatorship with the assistance of the few trusted journalists she knew.

In the middle of all the mayhem, Sofia and Alejandro were able to find a few seconds to themselves to collect their thoughts and regain their breath. They stood in front of a makeshift window and saw the city that they cared about as it moved beneath the cover of the night sky. In spite of the fact that there was peril lurking in the shadows, there was a sense of calm and the promise of a fresh morning.

"We did it," Sofia murmured in a voice that was scarcely audible above a whisper. "We were able to complete the task."

Alejandro cast a sideways glance in her direction, his mouth forming the beginnings of a grin. "Yes, we did," he said in response, shifting his attention back to the city. "But keep in mind that this is only the beginning. There is a great deal more work to be done."

The resolute expression on Sofia's face was reflected in her nod. "Then we'll do it together," the speaker said.

Their words lingered in the atmosphere, serving as a commitment that was just as binding as any oath. They were aware that the path that lay ahead of them was perilous. They, along with the lives of their fellow comrades, were in danger as a result of the retaliation that would be taken by the dictatorship. However, they kept their resolve. They had begun this conflict, and they intended to see it to a conclusion. The legend of the Phoenix was shown to be true, and now there was no turning back.

The subsequent few days were a whirlwind of activities that seemed to merge together. The initial shock caused by the disclosures about the corrupt nature of the leadership had caused waves of wrath and hatred to spread throughout the population. The previously carefully controlled metropolis was now a simmering stew of unrest that was on the verge of erupting into full-scale uprising.

During this period, Alejandro was operating at the height of his abilities, and the military acumen with which he had structured the rebel force became increasingly apparent. He divided the members into groups, and gave each group a specific set of responsibilities and an area of responsibility to work in. Others were in charge of rallying the residents and organizing peaceful protests, while a special team, which included Alejandro himself, was in charge of gathering intelligence and developing safety measures. Some were responsible for the acquisition of supplies and resources; others were in charge of mobilizing the citizens.

While Alejandro was in charge of operations, Sofia was responsible for maintaining communication. She put in a lot of hard effort to make sure that the people were kept informed about the actions of the dictatorship as well as the aims of the rebel organization. The message was disseminated far and wide thanks to Sofia's extensive network of journalists and informants, which she utilized when she began publishing a series of pieces that detailed the corruption that existed throughout the administration. Her writings became the voice of dissent, urging and motivating the populace to rise up against the repressive dictatorship.

They were able to use the radio frequency that they had previously acquired to good use at the same time. In the midst of the bleak circumstances, it functioned as a ray of light by providing the populace with information and messages. These updates were frequently provided by Alejandro, whose steady voice served to reaffirm their dedication to the cause, while Sofia's poetic words, when read aloud, reverberated across the city even during its sleepless evenings.

In spite of the hectic pace, Sofia and Alejandro discovered that being in one other's company brought them comfort. Their commitment to the same goal had brought them closer together, and as more time passed, their bond became stronger. They would frequently find themselves spending a calm time together in the midst of the bustle, even late into the night.

Their conversations ranged from heated arguments over their next step to reassuring words that they were heading in the right direction. These back-and-fourths were interspersed with grins and knowing looks from both parties. They had an understanding of one another's goals and anxieties, as well as their respective strengths and flaws. Their connection consisted of more than just friendship; it was also a commitment to one another as well as to the cause they supported.

As the days went on, they got increasingly brazen in their actions. The number of demonstrations increased, as did the level of anger among the population. Every successful mission, every broadcast, and every piece published dealt another blow to the dictatorship, slowly but gradually chipping away at their repressive control. The administration was on the defensive and desperately trying to recover control of the situation, but the tide was beginning to shift against them. The mythical phoenix was, in fact, making a comeback, and it was only a question of time before its raging fires consumed the repressive government.

The activities carried out by the insurgent organization were carried out with such pinpoint accuracy that it nearly looked unreal.

The manner in which each member was taught as well as the manner in which each mission was carried out was clear evidence of Alejandro's skill in the military. In the midst of the mayhem, they followed his tactical genius like a lighthouse thanks to the fact that he was a leader who was both authoritative and compassionate.

Alejandro spent his days attending meetings to discuss strategies, organizing mission itineraries, and making sure that their group was secure. His evenings were spent working on his surveillance skills or participating in training sessions. His commitment to the reason never wavered in the slightest. He was aware of the consequences that would result from their failure, and he was adamant that he would not allow them to occur.

The ensemble gradually became more careful as a result of Alejandro's influence. Everyone was aware of their role, as well as the time and location of their respective activities. It was just like a well-rehearsed dance, with each movement being precise and perfectly timed with the others. Alejandro took care to make sure that everybody was ready for everything that may happen. The rebels were trained to deal with any situation that may arise, including the use of weapons and basic first aid.

While Alejandro was in control of the more strategic aspects of the situation, Sofia was in charge of the narrative. Her ability to put her thoughts on paper helped give the uprising a voice. Her journalistic abilities shined through in the manner in which she produced each item of news and each broadcast. She gave a clear image of the corruption that was prevalent under the administration, as well as the desire of the rebel organization to fight for justice.

However, Sofia's part in the story did not end there. She made frequent trips to the locations of peaceful demonstrations, where she boosted the spirit of the locals. She was always there, standing side by side with the people and raising her voice along with them. She was an ever-present presence. She was not only a reporter covering the uprising; rather, Sofia was an active participant in the uprising herself.

In spite of the increasing amount of strain, Sofia and Alejandro discovered that their relationship gave them strength. The comfort they found in one another during their late-night gatherings. They found solace in the silent moments they shared together, in knowing looks, and in words of support whispered to one another. Their connection became stronger, which shone like a ray of light in the middle of the mounting anxiety.

The actions of the rebel organization were no longer being conducted in secret. They were bold and performed in public. Each assignment that they completed without incident served as a testament to their determination. The citizenry, who had been obedient in the past, were now participating in the uprising. They put up a fight, put up a resistance, and put up a fight. The city, which had been completely silent before, was suddenly filled with the yells of rebels.

The dictatorship was shaken to its foundations. They strained to keep their iron grip on the situation, which was beginning to show signs of slipping. However, the Phoenix had already risen from the ashes when they were discovered. The sparks of discontent continued to grow, and there was no indication that they would ever die out. The people in power were placed on notice that the uprising was not going away anytime soon.

Alejandro, Sofia, and the others persisted in their mission in spite of the dangers they faced on a regular basis because they were certain that the cause they were fighting for was right. The public were spurred into action as a result of Sofia's remarks, and her writings revealed the extent of greed and corruption inside the administration. It was rumored that these things were true, but they were never proven, and the stories were passed down in hushed tones in the shadows. Now everyone knew about them since they were published on underground news websites and discussed in the privacy of people's homes across the country.

The insurgent group, which Alejandro was strategically leading, carried on with their operations, making each one more audacious than the one before it. Their objectives shifted from simple outposts to important government buildings throughout the course of the conflict. Their covert assaults were launched on critical infrastructure like as power plants, communication towers, and armament storage sites.

The extensive understanding of military strategy that Alejandro possessed was extremely important. Each operation was a calculated risk, planned with precision to exploit any holes that Alejandro had detected in the regime's defenses, and carried out with the intention of taking advantage of those vulnerabilities. They moved like shadows, making their presence known only when they wanted it to be, and they left a swath of chaos in their wake as they went.

When they were finally successful in breaking into the communication network used by the government, this marked a critical turning point. The normally muffled airways were suddenly filled with Sofia's voice as she read her most recent essay, in which she detailed the transgressions of the dictatorship and their ill-gotten money, followed by a straightforward and uncompromising call to the people to stand against the oppressors.

The mission was fraught with peril, and on more than one occasion, Alejandro and his team found themselves in a confined space. Despite this, they prevailed thanks to their dogged perseverance and Alejandro's mastery of the strategic situation. The group as a whole had a few injuries, but there were no fatalities. Each brush with death served as a sobering reminder of the perils they were up against; nonetheless, it only seemed to reinforce their determination.

Their actions had begun to appear in news outlets all around the world. The pieces that Sofia wrote were circulated all across the world, and as a result, everyone started paying attention. The dictatorship found itself under a level of scrutiny it had never seen before, and human rights organizations started demanding action from their respective governments. International sanctions were also brought up around this time.

The dissatisfaction among the population was further exacerbated by all of these events. The formerly terrified public looked to the rebels as a glimmer of hope at this point in time. The seeds of discontent had not only taken root, but they were also beginning to develop into a strong opposition. Every action they took and every article they published brought them one step closer to their ultimate objective, which was to be free from oppression.

However, along with increased success came an increase in danger. The regime was on high alert at this point, and their actions were more circumspect. It became a game of cat and mouse, with the stakes being raised to their highest level. Nevertheless, even in the middle of this risky dance, the rebels, who were being led by Alejandro and Sofia, remained unshaken, their spirits remaining as uncompromising as ever. They had witnessed the beginning of the transformation that was to come. They were at this point tasked with ensuring that the fire would remain lit.

The inner workings of the rebel organization changed as the rebels continued to wage their war of disruption and truth while it was ongoing. What had first been an unorganized collection of dissidents who were enraged and despondent had, with the passage of time, developed into a well-oiled machine of opposition. No longer only anonymous faces in the crowd, Sofia, Alejandro, and the others quickly became familiar. They were leaders, which meant that their opinions had weight, and their judgments determined the path that their struggle would take.

Because of his extensive experience in the military, Alejandro acted as the group's primary strategist. He monitored every activity, his eyes scouring maps and plans while his mind calculated dangers and devised countermeasures. He was in charge of everything. His attention was directed on the wider picture, namely making certain that their efforts brought about genuine change and put the government on the defensive. Despite this, he did not try to remove himself from the activities on the ground. He was there, commanding his squad, making sure that every member got it back safely, and he was on the front lines.

On the other hand, Sofia battled with her writing, and it was her words that served as the gasoline that kept the flame of revolt burning strong. She was no longer simply a journalist; rather, she had become a ray of light and a voice for those who had been hushed. Every new piece of writing that she produced was more penetrating and illuminating than the one before it. She revealed the falsehoods, corruption, and greed that were at the root of the dictatorship and held all of these things up to the glaring light of the truth.

Her pieces were no longer merely reports; rather, they were summons to arms, imploring the populace to acknowledge the truth and to pursue justice. Additionally, they were successful. The people were no longer content to only observe the development of the uprising in a receptive manner; rather, they were actively participating in it, their fury mounting and their voices rising in unison in opposition to the dictatorship.

In addition, the covert activities got increasingly daring as time went on. The rebels were successful in infiltrating government buildings, where they damaged important infrastructure and intercepted top-secret communications. These were dangerous endeavors, and every accomplishment brought with it the scrumptious flavor of victory, while every failure brought with it the acrid pain of loss. There were contacts with the military that left them gasping for air and more conscious of the precarious nature of their life. There were near-death experiences. Despite this, they continued forth.

However, the success of their operative activities was not the only factor that determined their level of development. The insurgents were also prevailing in the struggle for the hearts and minds of the people. People started to join them, volunteers who donated their talents and time, fueled by the same passion and desire for change as the original group. With each new recruit, each successful operation, and each scandal that was uncovered, the regime's grasp on the country became a little bit weaker.

Despite this, the regime did not take a passive stance. It clenched its hand around the nation, and its desperation became increasingly apparent in the rising levels of violence and repression. The number of raids and curfews went up, the propaganda got more intense, and

the punishments for dissension became more severe. The possibility
of being found out and the repercussions that might follow it hung
large over the rebels. Each and every operation, as well as each and
every broadcast, was fraught with the possibility of being captured,
tortured, or even worse.

But despite this, they had a plan, and they were determined to
stick to it, despite the fact that they were afraid of what may happen.
The path that lay ahead of them was loaded with peril, but they were
certain that they had roused something tremendous within the
populace, a feeling of empowerment that could not be extinguished
no matter what. Their uprising was no longer simply a war; rather, it
was a dance of defiance against oppression, which served as a
demonstration of the tenacity of the human spirit. And as they
moved, the shadows of their anxieties began to disappear, and a new
dawn of optimism began to emerge in its stead.

Due to the increased magnitude of the activities, more structure
and resources were required than previously. As a result, Alejandro
was put in charge of handling the logistics of their operations and
painstakingly organizing every aspect. He considered it as a crucial
aspect of their ability to survive, in contrast to the perspective of
some of the other people in the group who saw it as a laborious
procedure. Because of the increasingly hazardous nature of their
business, even the smallest error might have catastrophic
consequences. Even though they possessed the advantage of surprise,
Alejandro realized that it wasn't enough for them to rely on alone.

In spite of the fact that the risks were getting higher, Alejandro
realized that he was becoming increasingly involved in the cause. He
spent his nights planning and coming up with new ideas, which
prevented him from falling or staying asleep most of the time. His
days were filled with a whirlwind of activity as he planned the next
steps, scouted for information, and trained the new recruits.
Whenever there was an operation taking place, his heart skipped a
beat, and the worry that he would hurt or kill someone was a
persistent and menacing thought that persisted in the back of his
mind at all times.

In the meanwhile, Sofia discovered that her journalistic instincts were developing. She was no longer only a bystander; rather, she had become a participant in the story. Every piece that she produced was not simply about exposing the tyranny; rather, it was also about capturing the spirit of the uprising, the tenacity, and the resolve of people fighting for their freedom.

Her work was done in secret at this point, under a series of aliases that shifted about as frequently as the wind. Even though each new piece posed a threat and offered the government another opportunity to track her down, she did not let this dissuade her. The more she wrote, the more she became aware of the power that might be harnessed via her words. They had the ability to incite people, make them rethink things, and provoke conflict. No longer simply Sofia, the journalist, she was now also Sofia, the revolutionary.

On the other hand, the operations and publications were not the only things that kept the insurrection going. Additionally, it was the people and the residents who began to come together in support of their cause. Some people offered them food and a place to stay, while others offered their talents, which ranged from computer hacking to medical expertise. These ordinary people were instrumental in keeping the momentum and morale of the uprising going strong. The seeds of revolt planted by Alejandro and Sofia were steadily blossoming into a widespread movement. Every operation provoked greater resentment among the population, and every uncovered scandal turned more residents against the dictatorship.

Despite this, there was a rise in risk as a direct result of the expansion of assistance. As the leadership became more conscious of the mounting dissent, it began to implement harsher repressive measures. In an effort to retake command of the situation, certain areas were given a military presence, curfews were instituted, and censorship was carried out. Although there was a greater chance than ever before of the rebels being detected, they did not give up.

It seemed fitting that the rebel movement be represented by the Phoenix, which is a symbol of rebirth. It was a demonstration of their resiliency, specifically their capacity to emerge from adversity more courageous and powerful. They were prepared to struggle for a better society, one that was free from the iron grasp of the dictatorship, and they dared to dream of a future that was better than the one that existed at the time.

Their shenanigans got more audacious, their actions riskier, and their determination more steadfast. The game of deceit was in full swing, a game that was morphing into a symphony of defiance, with each operation contributing a new note to the ever-increasing crescendo. The uprising was no longer a far-off possibility; rather, it had become a palpable fact, a flame that once lighted could not be quenched. The Phoenix did in fact begin to reappear, its wings of insurrection spreading out in all directions and throwing lengthy shadows over the government.

During this time period, a significant turn of events took place. The rebels have been in communication with a person with inside knowledge of the regime. The individual, who was a mid-level functionary at the ministry of defense and went under the moniker "Mariposa," started providing the insurgents with vital intelligence. Because of the knowledge he gave, the insurgents were able to execute more targeted attacks and steer clear of unanticipated head-on collisions. His contributions were of immense value.

The addition of this additional asset improved Sofia's reporting capabilities. Because of Mariposa's knowledge, she had access to more material than ever before, as well as hitherto unattainable facts on the dictatorship. By carefully constructing her pieces to illustrate the scope of the regime's wrongdoing while safeguarding her source, Sofia was able to expose corruption at a high level and bring the perpetrators to justice.

The general population was rocked to its core by these shocking findings. People who had previously backed the dictatorship, or at the very least, stayed neutral, started having second thoughts about their allegiances. The pieces written by Sofia quickly became the talk of the town. The citizens would hand out paper copies to one another while simultaneously rumoring about the concealed corruption in their administration. In public places, quiet voices discussed the specifics of the situation. The words said by Sofia were having the desired effect, planting the seeds of skepticism and wrath in the minds of the population.

While this was going on, Alejandro was constantly attempting to improve the approach that the gang was using. Using the intelligence that Mariposa provided, he coordinated attacks on government assets with the goal of reducing the regime's resources and bringing down its morale. Under Alejandro's direction, the rebel band was transforming into a well-organized militia bit by bit throughout the course of the conflict. Everything was starting to take on a more regimented form: training schedules, emergency procedures, and communication protocols.

In addition to this, Alejandro started building relationships with other rebel groups located all around the city. The dictatorship faced a more difficult adversary as a result of this network of opposition, which increased both their power and their access to resources. Each cell preserved its autonomy while cooperating with the others on crucial objectives and exchanging information and resources when it was important to do so.

During one of these operations, the insurgents were successful in stopping a large shipment of weaponry. The mission was high-stakes and included a number of different rebel groups; but, because to Alejandro's meticulous preparation and the intel provided by Mariposa, it was eventually successful. The cells received a considerable increase in their firepower as a result of the distribution of the captured weapons among them.

These triumphs, however, were tempered by a threat that was always lurking in the background: the rising violence of the government. As more evidence of corruption surfaced, the regime's control became increasingly oppressive. The frequency of public executions increased, serving as a chilling deterrent to anybody who may challenge the rule. It was not uncommon for innocent civilians to get caught in the crossfire and have their lives cut short just because they were in the wrong location at the wrong time.

Alejandro and Sofia, along with the other members of the rebel group, were required to proceed with more caution. Every action they took needed to be carefully analyzed, and each step of their strategy had to be carefully mapped out. Even a small mistake on their part may result in their capture or, even worse, their death.

The Phoenix did in fact begin to rise, but the shadows it cast became more ominous as it did so. The reply from the dictatorship served as a vivid reminder of the harsh reality that they were up against. Despite this, they continued on nonetheless. Their strategies got more audacious, and their determination became greater. They were engaging in risky behavior, engaging in deceptive dancing, and fighting for their independence all at the same time. And there was no sign of a retreat from their position.

In the midst of the escalation, Sofia's journalistic savvy started shifting gears in response to the developing situation. She went beyond merely reporting the facts about the wrongdoing and began writing emotional editorials. She wrote on the bravery of average folks as well as the spirit of resistance that was percolating just below the surface. She wrote about a nation that, in her mind, had the potential to be reborn from the ashes like a phoenix, purified by the flames of revolution, and more powerful and liberated than ever before. Her remarks added gasoline to the fire, igniting a sense of optimism and solidarity among the people of the community.

Despite the fact that her real identity was kept hidden from the general public, she became a symbol of the resistance as a result of the perilous circumstances in which she found herself. She became a symbol of the fight for independence, and her pen name, "La Voz," was spoken of with reverence at secret gatherings and dialogues that took place in alleyways.

In the meanwhile, Alejandro focused his efforts on ensuring that the insurgent organization would be able to continue existing. He took steps to guarantee that the organization would be able to continue functioning normally even in the event that key members were compromised. He came up with fail-safes, backup plans, and processes to make sure that each cell could function independently in the event that it was necessary. In addition to this, he took safety measures to safeguard Mariposa, their vital inside source.

In addition, Alejandro started instructing the rebels in hand-to-hand combat, which was an important skill set to have in the event that ammunition became limited. He shared with them strategies and methods that he had learned during his time in the military, which he believed would give them an advantage in difficult circumstances. Everyone was pushed to their limits during the arduous training sessions; nonetheless, they gladly put themselves through this ordeal since they were well aware of the importance of the task at hand.

The rebel group's morale remained strong despite the mounting threat despite the rising risk. They rejoiced in their accomplishments, drawing inspiration for further action from each successful mission. In the face of insurmountable obstacles, their sense of camaraderie served as their strength, and the common goal of establishing a free nation served to knit them together.

There were also casualties, as several of their allies were taken prisoner or murdered during the conflict. Each death was lamented in great depth, serving as a sobering reminder of the treacherous foe they were up against. Despite this, their resolve simply became stronger after each defeat. The prize was substantial, which was the liberty of their people, but the risk was significant as well.

They began to recognize a change in the mood of the city as their behaviors became increasingly defiant over the course of time. The populace, who had previously been afraid and repressed, started exhibiting symptoms of unrest. The revelations made by Sofia, in conjunction with the actual effects brought about by the actions of the rebels, were causing a palpable sense of disquiet among the populace.

The city was on the verge of exploding like a powder keg, with the level of anxiety rising with each passing day. People in the community who had previously chosen to ignore what was going on are now extending their homes to fleeing rebels. On walls all across the city, spray paint was sprayed with the phrase "La Voz speaks for us," and it quickly spread. There were visible fissures forming in the formerly impregnable control that the dictatorship had over the city. The regime's grip on the city was beginning to weaken.

However, as the strength of the opposition increased, so did the efforts of the dictatorship to put an end to it. The rebels were not naive about the path that lay in wait for them; they were well aware of it. The road to freedom was riddled with peril, and it required making sacrifices along the way. But for Alejandro, Sofia, and the rest of the rebels, the battle had become much more than a cause; it was their very lifeblood, and it was their shared goal of a new dawn for their nation. They were not only existing under the tyranny of the dictatorship; rather, they were actively resisting it. Their spirits remained unbroken as they rose from the ashes, much like the phoenix that symbolized their defiance.

The number of days turned into weeks, and the weeks turned into months, but the rebel squad, commanded by Alejandro, kept pushing forward regardless of the passage of time. Their efforts, which were unorganized and unsophisticated at one point, had developed into a sophisticated campaign of resistance over time. Alejandro's keen strategic mind made certain that they were always one step ahead of the government, and he ensured this by planning each operation with painstaking attention to detail.

They started going after the regime's resources because they were aware that in order to bring the regime's activities to a halt, they needed to cut it off from its lifeblood. Using their inside information to its fullest potential, they attacked supply convoys, warehouses, and ammunition stockpiles. The brazen strikes carried out by the rebels not only had an effect on the operations of the dictatorship, but they also served to further excite the populace, with their brave acts becoming legendary among the residents of the city.

Her journalistic work continued to incite discontent among members of the general public, and Sofia remained the voice of this burgeoning uprising. Her writings served as a rallying call for those who had the audacity to dream for a brighter future, and each exposé that she published was more devastating than the one before it. Her impassioned articles lauded the bravery of the insurgent group, praising them for their stance against the dictatorship and lauding their dogged pursuit of justice. She urged the people to rise up against the oppression of the dictatorship and underlined the need of the population maintaining their solidarity and fortifying their resolve.

During the time that Alejandro and Sofia were devoting more and more of themselves to their cause, they also worked to strengthen their relationship. All of these experiences, including the shared peril, the late-night planning meetings, the victories and the losses, worked to establish a tie between them that was unbreakable. They discovered that being in each other's company was soothing, that their dreams were similar, and that they had a tremendous respect for the other person's tenacity and resolve.

But as their feelings for one another deepened, so did their anxiety at being parted. Each mission that they planned may turn out to be their last, and each farewell might turn out to be their very last. However, they did not allow their dread to stop them from proceeding. Instead, it helped to highlight how important their struggle was and how urgent their objective was becoming.

The uprising had evolved into something far more than a simple succession of activities. In contrast to the tyrannical rule of the dictatorship, it was a proclamation of human dignity and the right to live free from its shackles. And Alejandro and Sofia were at the center of it all, with their leadership igniting the passion of those around them and their unyielding determination stoking the fires of the uprising.

However, as the rebels gained more ground, the government became more determined than ever to put an end to their uprising. More soldiers were sent in, checkpoints and curfews were made stricter, and interrogations were conducted in a more severe manner. The dictatorship was no longer going to brush the uprising off as simple discontent; rather, it was beginning to acknowledge it as a genuine threat.

There were perils around every bend, and shadows lingered in every nook and cranny. Every day was a gamble, and every procedure was a dangerous tango with death. But the insurgent group persisted in their mission in spite of the dangers they faced, driven by the conviction that the cause they were fighting for was righteous and the sacrifices they were making were essential.

It appeared as though the phoenix was actually rising as the flames of the revolt continued to blaze brilliantly despite the gloom that pervaded the city.

As a result of Sofia's writings gaining popularity among civilians and non-compliant government employees alike, the city was filled with the resounding sound of a collective voice of defiance. The ambitious stories of the rebels' adventures produced vivid images in the imaginations of the readers, which fanned the smoldering fires of discontent into a burning yearning for change.

In the meantime, Alejandro was running the operations with a keen eye for detail and a strategic mind that was razor sharp. Each mission was precisely planned, and every danger was carefully evaluated and minimized, all in an effort to achieve maximum efficiency with the fewest possible deaths. He had honed his skills to the point where he was an expert at locating weak points in the defenses of the government and ruthlessly exploited those weaknesses to forward their cause. Every victory, regardless of how insignificant, dealt a blow to the repressive system.

The supply lines that had previously served as the regime's operational arteries were gradually being severed one at a time. As the munitions and supplies that were formerly housed in the warehouses have been reduced to ashes, the regime's grasp on power continues to weaken. They were able to execute these assaults with pinpoint accuracy and effectively avoid being captured because to Alejandro's knowledge of the organizational structure and strategies utilized by the military.

However, the conflicts were not confined to the arena of physical combat alone. On the information front, Sofia's efforts were just as significant and crucial. Her words struck with the might of a cannon, making her pen more powerful than any blade she could have wielded. Every item that she wrote tore the veils off the pretenses that the administration was maintaining and revealed the rot that was underlying. Once just the subject of hushed murmurs, the corrupt nature of the administration was now written down for all to see in plain and white. The residents were given a strong sense of validation and togetherness as a result of this transparency, which helped to further strengthen the cause of the insurrection.

In the midst of all the chaos, Alejandro and Sofia felt that their connection was growing stronger. They were two parts of a whole, leading their people's attack against those who oppressed them collectively. The difficulties that they had to overcome together had elevated their original regard for one another and their sense of camaraderie to a higher, more meaningful level. It was an affection that was fashioned in the fiery furnace of struggle, an unspoken understanding that they were each other's pillars of strength in this taxing fight.

The fact that they were becoming closer to one another, however, brought with it the risk of losing one another, which made their successes feel that much more excruciating. Every mission that they undertook had the possibility of being their last, which was a sobering reminder of how much was riding on the outcome of their uprising. However, they did not allow fear to stop them from proceeding. Each near-miss with peril helped to further solidify their belief, as well as their determination, to fight for a future in which they would be able to live in peace, unfettered by oppression.

The regime, which had first shown little concern for the insurgents, was now visibly shaken. Its replies became increasingly angry and frantic as time went on. The city was subjected to an onslaught of crackdowns, checkpoints were increased in number, and curfews were made more stringent. More troops were sent out to monitor the streets, and their presence served as a continual reminder of the regime's intention to put down any indication of revolt that may arise.

In spite of the worsening situation, the rebel group continued to make progress, much like the legendary bird, the phoenix. Their fearless determination was unshaken in the face of the growing number of obstacles. Every calculated risk they took and strategic action they took got them one step closer to achieving their objective, which was to bring back freedom and justice to their city. Their uprising had turned into a shining example of what might be accomplished through the power of collaboration and fortitude in the face of insurmountable obstacles.

Alejandro and Sofia maintained their composure despite the turbulent events that were taking place in this new chapter of their lives. Each operation carried out by the rebels is evidence of their tenacity, and the rebels continued to chip away at the authority held by the state under Alejandro's skillful guidance. Through her writing, Sofia exposed the corrupt practices of the administration, therefore motivating the populace, planting the seeds of discontent, and ultimately igniting the fires of insurrection.

They shattered the foundations of the dictatorship with every fight that they fought and every word that they spoke, each action being a rebellion against the persecution. Their bravery was a lighthouse that guided the inhabitants out of the darkness and stoked the fire of hope that was already there in their hearts.

However, the increasing stakes acted as a glaring reminder of the dangerous nature of the route that they were traveling. The regime's crackdowns became increasingly brutal, and its desperation was clear for all to see. However, they did not allow their bravery to waver. They proceeded forth with unwavering determination in spite of the impending threat and the overwhelming odds against them.

The city held its breath as the hazardous game of cat and mouse between the rebels and the dictatorship proceeded. It was a ballet of deceit, and it was keeping everyone in the city guessing. In spite of not knowing what was about to happen, there was an odd sense of expectancy in the air. The populace watched as the rebels pursued their audacious plan while their emotions were simultaneously filled with hope and terror.

As the sun went down over the city, it formed lengthy shadows that seemed to reflect the difficulties faced by the people who lived there. The day came to a close, and with it, this particular chapter in each of their lives, but the narrative was not yet over. The fact that they persisted during the conflict is evidence of both their tenacity and the strength of the people. In spite of the chaos, one thing was abundantly clear: the Phoenix had, in fact, risen, and it was prepared to engage in the fights that were still to come.

CHAPTER 9 "NIGHT OF THE LONG KNIVES"

Tensions were running high across the city. Even while the phoenix may have risen from the ashes, the government, which was determined to maintain its grip on power, was not about to let it fly free.

The week had been peaceful. The unsettling hush that had descended over the city was much more unsettling than its customary din. It was like an electric charge was hanging in the air, and Sofia could feel a feeling of impending dread. She could feel the quiet before the storm. Even Alejandro, who had a history in the military, was able to recognize the shift in the water's level, and the rebel group made preparations for the storm that they knew was on the horizon.

Although the government had been silent, they were certainly not doing nothing. They had been passing the time by observing, waiting, and plotting their revenge during this period of time. General Montoya, the regime's iron hand, had been secretly gathering his soldiers in the shadows all this time. Montoya was a tough opponent, and the rebels were well aware of his reputation for both the ruthlessness of his methods and the genius of his strategic thinking.

When the storm eventually began in earnest, it was a far more severe occurrence than any of them had anticipated. It was a comprehensive, violent campaign that was aimed to eliminate the rebel organization once and for all. The operation was given the code name "Night of the Long Knives," and it was dubbed "Night of the Long Knives." The armies of the dictatorship fell upon the city like a swarm, their numbers being overpowering and their weaponry being unmatched by anything else.

It was a night filled with mayhem and bloodshed. The streets were abandoned, and the only sounds that could be heard were the sounds of gunfire echoing through the empty streets. The air was thick with tension, and the smell of smoke and terror filled the air. The soldiers of the government marched into the city, the darkness of their uniforms providing a striking contrast to the flames that blazed all around them. The insurgents put up a brave fight, despite the fact that they were severely outnumbered.

In all of their training, there was just no way that they could have been ready for the sheer enormity of the attack. They suffered a devastating defeat, and their numbers continued to dwindle with each passing minute. Even though Alejandro was a skilled tactician and commanded his troops with unyielding determination, he was unable to alter the course of the battle. The conflict was vicious and cruel to both sides. As a result of the regime's unrelenting efforts, the rebels were forced back and eventually surrounded.

In the meantime, Sofia made use of her instincts as a journalist to find her way through the maze-like city, eluding arrest while reporting on the bloodshed that was taking on all around her. The residents of the city, who had been agitated and hungry for change in the past, were suddenly rendered helpless as a result of the brutal response of the dictatorship. As the predicament continued to deteriorate, Sofia became aware that the night was not just a battle for the insurgents, but also a battle for the very essence of their city.

After a number of hours had passed, the insurgents eventually found themselves trapped with their backs against a wall. However, despite the fact that the odds were stacked against them, they did not give up. They would defend their city and their house with their very last breath since this was their city and their home. This night was their "Night of the Long Knives," a night filled with peril and despair, a night in which every second was a battle for survival.

In spite of the upheaval occurring outside, there was an eerie calm within the hideout that the rebels had constructed for themselves deep beneath the maze-like streets of the city. It was in this location that Alejandro saw Sofia frantically working on her worn-out laptop, her face lit by the harsh brightness emanating from the screen. Her fingers moved as quickly as lightning as she determinedly documented the atrocities that had occurred during the night.

As Alejandro observed her, he couldn't help but feel a twinge of appreciation in his chest. In the middle of the mayhem, Sofia served as a guiding light for them, and her words served as their most effective weapon. Despite this, he was aware of the psychological strain that it had on her as a result of her having to see such unrelenting savagery. In the middle of the loud clamor of the conflict, he came to her side and placed a reassuring hand on her shoulder as an unspoken assurance of support.

The conflict continued in the public areas, such as the streets. Even though they were severely injured, Alejandro's crew was not yet defeated. They battled in pockets, adopting various guerilla techniques that they had learned from Alejandro. Every back street was turned into a battlefield, and every darkness hid a possible danger. The formerly familiar city has been transformed into a perilous labyrinth, with its walls drawing closer together.

The determination of the insurgents was unshakeable throughout the slaughter. They were the city's beating heart, beating with a life that was rebellious in the face of the regime's iron hold. Every shot fired and every life put in danger worked to chip away at the regime's outward appearance of invulnerability, planting the seeds of uncertainty inside its ranks.

Despite this, as the night wore on, the number of rebels continued to decrease. They found themselves repeatedly pushed back, besieged, as their run-ins with the regime's soldiers became increasingly regular and intense. It appeared as though the regime had been tracking their activities, learning their techniques, and attempting to anticipate their next actions. It was a game of cat and mouse, and the cat was getting closer all the time.

A race against the clock was being run by Sofia. The majority of the city's communications had been disrupted as a result of the regime's effective jamming, but Sofia had been prepared for this. She was able to disseminate a stream of information, exposing the horrors committed by the dictatorship, by employing a primitive, improvised transmitter. Her comments were the only way for the city to communicate with the outside world and a plea for assistance, but she was well aware that it was only a matter of time until the government discovered the origin of the transmission and tracked it back to her.

As the night progressed until the early hours of the morning, the situation for the rebels became more and more hopeless. Alejandro, ever the master planner, was well aware of the precarious situation they were in. Despite this, he refused to accept that he had lost. This was their city, and this was their struggle; they were prepared to take on whatever that came their way. During the "Night of the Long Knives," even though there was a palpable sense of hopelessness in the air, the rebels clung to hope with all their might since it was the only thing they had left.

During those grueling hours just before dawn, it appeared as though the city was holding its breath in preparation for the decisive onslaught. The regime's soldiers were like a relentless wave sweeping in on the remaining strongholds of the revolt, and the buzz of approaching military vehicles became louder and louder as it echoed through the vacant streets.

As Alejandro stood among his fatigued warriors, the occasional flashes of light from the explosions in the distance highlighted their features. It became increasingly difficult to withstand the anxiety as time went on. Despite the fact that he was aware that they were outgunned, outnumbered, and surrounded, he met the gaze of each of his companions with grim determination. He was the one who led them into this conflict, and he would also be the one to guide them through whatever was ahead.

After taking a few deep breaths, Sofia sent her final broadcast into the ether, which was a pleading message that reverberated across the eerie quiet of the beleaguered city. Her remarks were no longer merely a report; rather, they were a testimony of their fight, a record of their defiance, and maybe a eulogy for those who had lost their lives. Even though the future was precariously balanced on the edge of a cliff, she immortalized their unconquerable sprit in the annals of history with each word that she spoke.

The rebels braced themselves for what they knew was about to happen as the first light of morning began to shine through the streets that were littered with wreckage. The "Night of the Long Knives" would be known for all time as a night of grim resolve and violent warfare, a night that served as a monument to their defiance. A night in which the spirit of the city, while being confronted with overwhelming odds, refused to bend down before the power of a ruler.

Even in this most difficult time, there was a peculiar and gloomy sense of triumph among the rebels. They would always be remembered by the city and the people who lived there, no matter what the future held for them. Their defiance had provided the tinder needed to start a fire, and the rebellion's origins had been firmly planted. And even in the event that they were to be defeated right now, their legacy would continue on.

As the last words fade into the void, the shattered city waits for the dawn, and the tale of Alejandro and Sofia and their unstoppable uprising lives on. The stage is now ready for the next act of their fight, which will find them balancing on the precipice between hopelessness and courage, submission and defiance.

CHAPTER 10 "ECHOES OF THE LOST EDEN"

During the dark hours of the morning that followed the 'Night of the Long Knives.' The remaining rebels, including Alejandro and Sofia, have been driven back to their last bastion, which was once a beautiful colonial-era home but is now scorched and damaged as a result of the battle. This deteriorating structure has become their final stronghold, their Eden in the midst of a metropolis that has been destroyed by the repressive policies of the dictatorship.

Since they have no other choice, the rebels decide to take a stand. In spite of the overwhelming challenges, Alejandro leads the defense with a steely determination. The stately home is transformed into an improbable stronghold through the use of every nook and cranny, as well as each and every stairway and room. She promotes their narrative, reaching out to the masses and converting their hopeless stance into a rallying cry. Sofia's eyes are tired but she remains stubborn.

The anxiety levels are rising as the day transitions into the evening. The forces loyal to the dictatorship are getting closer. In the waning light, battle-weary troops with emotionless features are getting ready to charge the mansion. Their weapons are gleaming. The will of the rebel to fight does not waver in the face of the assault.

The assault starts with a terrifying cacophony of gunshots and explosions, which can only be described as a deafening roar. In the face of the enormous might possessed by the dictatorship, Alejandro leads his forces in a battle with the ferocity of an animal that has been trapped. Her words reverberate through the deserted streets like a lighthouse in the midst of the roaring storm as Sofia relays the events of the ongoing fight to the city via an outdated and worn-out transmitter.

Something remarkable takes place in the middle of the never-ending mayhem. The ordinary people are inspired to take action as a result of Sofia's broadcasts, which result in a wave of citizen uprisings around the city. What began as a final stand for a tiny handful of rebels has grown into a revolt that spans the all of the city, an insurrection that the troops of the dictatorship weren't prepared for. After hearing of the bravery and perseverance of their unsung heroes, the general populace musters the willpower to stand up to their oppressors.

The conflict continues throughout the night, with the house serving as an isolated isle in the midst of the upheaval caused by the revolution. The morning carries with it the echoes of Eden, both the Eden that was lost and the Eden that was found. The formerly unstoppable forces of the dictatorship fall apart under the pressure of the combined efforts of the rebels and the rebellion of the civilian population. The regime that had been ruling with an iron hand has been toppled.

The next morning presents a picture of a Venezuela that is beginning to emerge from its long slumber. The city has taken a beating but has not been completely destroyed. The phoenix-like ascent of the spirit of freedom from the ashes and wreckage of its former home is powerful and relentless. Alejandro and Sofia, the improbable leaders of this uprising, are shown standing tall amidst the wreckage of their former stronghold as they observe the beginning of a new era.

When they take in the sight of their city, the place they've called home for as long as they can remember, it fills their emotions with an overpowering mixture of relief and anguish, triumph and loss. The conflict for Venezuela had come to an end. The battle for its existence, on the other hand, had just begun.

As a result of the brutal revolution, the people of Caracas have started picking up the pieces of both their city and their lives in order to start over. The streets are being cleaned up, the rubble is being swept away, and the eerie echoes of shooting are being gradually replaced by the sounds of hammering and building. Alejandro, Sofia, and the other members of the resistance immerse themselves into this process, contributing to the healing of the city, which had become a battlefield for their frantic war.

Every day presents its own unique set of obstacles and

accomplishments, from something as simple as a cleaned roadway to something as monumental as a reopened market. Food, which was difficult to come by during the worst of the regime's authority, starts to flow more freely as local sellers risk selling their products on the highways that have been restored. The skeleton of the city itself eventually regains flesh and vitality as the frames of buildings that were once only skeletons are gradually filled out with bricks and concrete.

In the middle of the reconstruction, Alejandro works very hard to construct a new military system that is both of the people and for the people. His prior position in the regime's armed forces provides him with the expertise necessary to lead, but it is his comprehension of the suffering of the people that drives him to make judgments. In order to prevent a recurrence of the atrocities committed in the past, he instills a respect for one's fellow people in his newly formed police force.

In the meanwhile, Sofia has become a powerful voice for the people, and the attention that her reports receive is widespread. She keeps broadcasting despite the fact that her voice is no longer a helpless wail in the night but rather a guiding light for the revival of Venezuela. The journalistic work that Sofia does leans more toward the upbeat and optimistic, concentrating on tales of perseverance and rebirth. Despite this, she does not shy away from the challenges that are still there; rather, she gives voice to the battles that endure even in the wake of the revolution.

As more time passes, the wounds left by the struggle begin to heal, and in their place is the vibrant pulse of a city that has been resurrected. In the middle of the revitalization of their country, Alejandro and Sofia take solace in the fact that their relationship is becoming stronger as a result of the experiences they have had in common. Their mutual affection eventually blossoms into love, a robust and profound bond that is created amid the fires of revolutionary conflict.

Nevertheless, even in the midst of all this revitalization, a real feeling of loss can be felt. The price of their newly discovered liberty was costly, since it was paid for with the blood and lives of their fellow soldiers. In memory of the valiant individuals who battled and sacrificed their lives during the uprising, memorials are being erected all across the city. Their names continue to reverberate throughout the core of the city, serving as a continual reminder of the cost of liberty.

Even though the community is still reeling from the loss, there is a growing sense of solidarity among its residents as a result of the tragedy. The people of Venezuela, whose will have been strengthened by the years they spent living under the government and by their battle for freedom, have come to share the goal of ensuring that such a period of oppression will never occur again. The collective spirit of resiliency and resolve is the most potent signal of the regeneration of the country, yet each day provides new physical evidence of development.

Alejandro, who is now a prominent figure in this new period, devotes his entire being to the process of reorganizing the military. He is responsible for organizing training programs that stress respect for human rights, discipline, and most crucially, the realization that the military is a servant of the people and not an instrument for tyranny of the populace. Every fresh recruit receives instruction on the harrowing events that occurred under the regime's rule and takes an oath to defend the nation and it's just won independence.

A loose confederation of decentralized news organizations starts to take form with Sofia acting as a guide. She makes sure that these organizations are founded on the truth and act in a transparent manner, which provides citizens with information that can be trusted. The persistent efforts that Sofia puts forth in order to educate and enlighten the people cultivate a sense of shared responsibility among the citizens, therefore producing an informed citizenry that is prepared to preserve its democracy.

During this time, efforts are being put toward the goal of building a new government. The process is difficult, as there will be disagreements on the structure, leadership, and the particulars of the constitution. These conversations include significant participation from Alejandro, Sofia, and the other leaders of the insurrection. They fight tooth and nail for a government that prioritizes the well-being of its citizens, keeps a close eye out for instances of corruption, and, most importantly, safeguards the liberties for which they have battled so valiantly.

In the late hours of one evening, Alejandro locates Sofia working in her improvised office. She is surrounded by piles of documents and screens that are flashing. He enters the room stealthily and then silently closes the door behind him. In the dim illumination of the room, Sofia raises her head, and the look in her eyes conveys an extreme level of tiredness. Alejandro leans closer to her while dragging a chair in for a closer conversation. On the desk, his hand approaches hers with the gentlest of touches despite the war scars it bears. Their common tiredness, the weight of their obligations, and the extent of their loss are all temporarily alleviated by this straightforward link between them.

The two leaders continue to talk late into the night about their aspirations for the future and the difficult responsibilities that lay in wait for them. Their collective hope for a free Venezuela, one in which repression is a thing of the past, serves as the gasoline that keeps them going strong. Alejandro and Sofia make a promise to commemorate the sacrifices of their dead friends as the sun begins to rise and casts the first light on a city that refuses to be broken. Alejandro and Sofia make the deal as the sun begins to rise and cast the first light on a city that refuses to be shattered. Their dedication is as unwavering as the morning light, even if the echoes of Eden's demise have been replaced by the noises of a phoenix rising from the ashes.

As the days pass into weeks, Alejandro, Sofia, and their other comrades continue to toil at around the clock to establish the framework for their new nation. The hopes and aspirations of the people are being woven into the fabric of a constitution that is starting to take form. There has been a proliferation of town halls around the city, each one humming with fervent conversations and heated disputes. Citizens, who had no voice while the dictatorship was in power, are suddenly given the opportunity to have a role in the destiny of their nation, which they seize with both hands.

The mental wounds are much deeper, despite the fact that the city's physical wounds are progressively healing. Throughout the city of Caracas, memorials have been built to honor the those who gave their lives during the uprising. They remain as somber reminders of the price that had to be paid in lives that will never be forgotten in order for them to gain their freedom.

The spirit of the Venezuelan people has not been shattered despite all of the suffering and difficulties they have endured. The remnants of the previous government are being gradually supplanted by emblems of perseverance and optimism. These structures, which were formerly damaged by gunfire, have been repurposed into centers for education and cultural activities. The footsteps of people and the sound of gunshots that used to reverberate through the streets have been replaced by the giggling of children at play, the murmur of ordinary conversations, and the rhythm of life moving ahead.

As a result of this change, Alejandro and Sofia's connection to one another grows stronger. They have a deep regard and affection for one another, as well as a common goal for a better future, which helps develop the close relationship that exists between them. Their company turns becomes an unsaid source of strength and a shelter for them in the midst of the unrelenting requirements of their new positions.

At some point during the day, Alejandro comes into Sofia while she is observing the city from a rooftop as the sun begins to set. The city is bathed in hues of orange and gold as a result of the warm glow, which also casts long shadows that appear to be reaching out, much as the people have, towards a more promising future. He approaches her and then joins her as she sits in silence to think about the city that they both adore.

As the sun sinks beyond the horizon, Sofia turns to look at Alejandro with a contemplative expression on her face. She talks about the transformation they've seen, the rebirth of a nation from its ashes, and the hope that today, despite everything, thrives in the hearts of their people. She also talks about the rebirth of a nation from its ashes. Alejandro listens, the emotions in his heart resonating with what she is saying. There, as the sun begins to set over Venezuela, they reaffirm their promise to devote the rest of their lives to serving the Venezuelan people.

Each new day provides its own unique set of difficulties, as well as a brand-new slate of chances to advance. Alejandro, Sofia, and the people of Venezuela face each day with unwavering determination, their spirits rising in defiance just as the sun rises each morning over the city that they hold dearest to their hearts. Their journey is not ended, and their suffering is not forgotten; nevertheless, with each stride they take, they move further away from the echoes of the lost Eden, and closer to a future that is full of hope and opportunity.

In the center of Caracas, among the buildings that still retain the wounds of the terrible history they have lived through, rumors are starting to circulate. There are stories spoken about shadows that lurk in the city's winding passageways and about unexpected faces that might be seen amid the throng. There is an increasing feeling of disquiet, as well as rumors that the remnants of the previous administration have begun to reunite, and that they are hiding out in the very heart of the city that they used to oppress.

The first time that Alejandro hears these stories, it is from one of his scouts, a young lady with keen eyes named Isabella. Isabella had been an important figure in the collecting of intelligence for the revolt. Her story is not reliable since it is based on piecemeal sightings and murmurs that are only partly heard, but it is plenty to make Alejandro uneasy. His stomach knots up with a feeling of dread he is all too acquainted with, memories of the violence of the government still fresh in his memory. The pledge that he will conduct an investigation, however, is accompanied by a steely resolve in his eyes.

During this time, Sofia is making her customary rounds among the city's many construction sites when she comes upon an oddity that catches her attention. A secret stockpile of weapons, some of which are brand new while others are unnervingly familiar, has been secreted away in the basement of an abandoned building. She hurriedly relayed the information to Alejandro despite her racing heart.

As the two individuals dig more into these unsettling facts, it becomes abundantly evident that they are in the midst of an immediate danger. It is no longer possible to brush off as mere hysteria rumors that former soldiers of the dictatorship are organizing a rebel movement in the middle of the city. The ghost of the Maduro regime, which was considered to be securely in the past, is now again throwing its menacing shadow on the present. This is a terrible revelation.

Their inquiries led them to a secret gathering of the reorganized soldiers, which was taking place in the cover of night at an old factory. Alejandro and Sofia watch from a concealed vantage point as individuals emerge from the darkness with the faint light making it difficult to make out their identity. They are being led by a man whose silhouette appears to be eerily recognizable; he is a specter from Venezuela's dark past.

They are knocked to their knees by the reality that dawns on them. It is true that the former dictatorship is reforming itself, and while it is doing it under a new banner, it nevertheless adheres to the same repressive ideals. The recollection of their cruel rule causes a sickening fear to well up in the very depths of their guts. In spite of this, an unshakable resolve begins to solidify inside both Alejandro and Sofia as the anxiety and uncertainty continues.

They had struggled in the past to free their country from the grasp of oppression and had succeeded. They would do it without any reservations the next time. Their voyage was not even close to being completed, and neither did it appear that their battle was. The phoenix that had been resurrected from the ashes was making preparations to once again protect its recreated Eden from the remnants of a long-forgotten history.

A shockwave was thrown through the newly constituted

administration as well as the population of the country when the announcement that Maduro's army had been reformed. Nevertheless, the lack of clarity regarding their goals was possibly the most troubling aspect of the situation. Were they putting together a resistance movement in preparation for an uprising? Or was their primary objective just to establish themselves as a strong challenge to the leadership that was already in place? These questions lingered heavily in the atmosphere, adding another layer of anxiety to a situation that was already in a perilous position.

Due to Alejandro's expertise in the military, he decided to do more information gathering on his own. He was well aware that gaining a knowledge of his adversary was of the utmost importance in order to protect his people. It turned out that Alejandro's connections within the city were essential, as they provided him with much-needed intelligence on the troops that were regrouping.

While Alejandro was doing his research, Sofia was doing everything she could to maintain the vitality of the spirit of their people. In the face of hardship, she wrote empowering essays that spoke of optimism, resilience, and the significance of solidarity in the community. She pleaded with the people of the country not to lose hope in the democracy for which they had worked so hard. Her comments conveyed this message. She underlined the need of being vigilant and strong, pleading with them not to allow fear to destroy the calm that had been so difficult to achieve.

In the meanwhile, Alejandro had been successful in confirming their most dire concerns. His clandestine investigations exposed the objective of the regrouped forces, which was to undermine the existing government in order to reclaim the authority they had previously had. It came out that the mysterious gentleman who was guiding them was General Armando Ortiz, a prominent actor in Maduro's leadership and a man known for his cruelty and cunning.

In light of this information, Alejandro and Sofia were aware that they needed to move quickly. They did not waste any time in reporting their results to the government and emphasized the importance of taking fast action. A clandestine emergency meeting was called to order. There, they spoke about different plans while assessing the risks and rewards of each conceivable course of action that may be taken.

Alejandro and Sofia decided to take matters into their own hands while the authorities deliberated about what course of action to take. They reached out in a stealthy manner to their reliable partners inside the uprising, cautioning them about the approaching threat and preparing them for the likelihood of yet another confrontation. Even though the news was shocking to their allies, they have assured them of their everlasting support. If conditions warranted it, the seeds of revolt that had been planted in the past were prepared to sprout once more.

Their conflict had not yet been resolved. Alejandro, Sofia, and the other people of Venezuela, along with the rest of the country's inhabitants, had bled and suffered far too much to allow those who intended to oppress them to regain control of their nation. They would brace themselves as the danger loomed over their heads, getting ready to fight with everything they had to protect the freedom they had just won. The echoes of the destroyed Eden were still audible, and the Phoenix stood poised, ready to rise once again in defiance of the oppressive forces.

After it was discovered that the troops of the previous administration who were reorganizing were not operating alone, the situation grew even more complicated. Informants of Alejandro's had begun to report the existence of foreign agents within the opposition; these agents could be distinguished from other opposition members by their strange accents and mannerisms. As time went on, it became abundantly evident that the forces that were reorganizing had partners in Cuba and Russia, who were supplying them with resources and giving them with strategic assistance. This brought an additional level of danger to an already precarious scenario, which raised the stakes to an even higher level.

Sofia, for her part, continued to rouse the public, and her journalism served as the beating heart of their fledgling democracy during this time. It wasn't long before her art captured the attention of people all across the world. Her unwavering commitment to telling the truth in her writing struck a chord with readers all around the world and made its way into the halls of power in Washington, DC.

The new democratic administration in Venezuela has received assistance from the United States government, which was moved to action by riveting articles written by Sofia that chronicle the fight of the Venezuelan people and their bravery. The decision to provide diplomatic and financial support to Sofia, Alejandro, and the rest of their fellow citizens was revealed at a high-profile news conference by the Secretary of State for the United States of America. The news was welcomed with a mixture of reactions, including relief and fear; although backing from a global power was heartening, it also served as a sharp reminder of the increasing gravity of their predicament.

Although the help from the United States was important, it did not come without its own unique set of difficulties. The negotiations were difficult because Alejandro and Sofia were working to guarantee that the assistance from the United States would not undermine the sovereignty of their nation. They emphasized that, while they were appreciative for the assistance, it was important to them to determine the course of the destiny of their nation on their own terms.

During the course of this unfolding geopolitical drama, Alejandro and Sofia bolstered their defensive positions. The insurgent organization, which forms the backbone of the country's armed forces at this point, ramped up their training. The fact that they were aware of the alliances formed by the adversary made them even more determined.

The public's disposition shifted as a result of the revelations regarding Cuba and Russia's participation. The residents, who had been reveling in the dawn of their newly discovered freedom, were hit with the harsh reality of the position in which they found themselves. This was the impetus that Sofia used to get her fellow residents to take action. She encouraged them to maintain their resolve and guard the democracy that they had helped to birth through her essays, which served as a gentle reminder of the sprit that had guided them during the revolution.

As the events continue to unfold, Venezuela, which is led by Alejandro and Sofia, is preparing for the conflicts that are still to come. The echoes of the paradise that had been lost had awoken the Phoenix, and now it was prepared to protect its nest against any danger that may arise. The war was no longer only about their nation; now, it was about their beliefs, their freedom, and the ability to choose their own path for the future.

The assistance that was provided by the United States of America served as a driving force behind unparalleled expansion. The majority of the financial support provided was put toward the reconstruction of the country's vital infrastructure, while diplomatic assistance helped open Venezuela up to global markets that it had been cut off from in the past owing to the actions of the previous administration. The economic impact was tangible, and within a few of months, a discernible uptick in the level of living was visible to everyone who cared to look.

However, despite the encouraging developments, there was a noticeable level of anxiety in the air. As the new leader of the Venezuelan military, Alejandro had to strike a balance between the requirements of training new recruits, maintaining a high level of morale, and navigating the political complexities of their international partners. Every day was a challenge to his tactical prowess, a balancing act on the precipice of disaster.

He maintained frequent contact with military advisors from the United States and utilized their knowledge to develop their motley rebel outfit into a professional army that is equipped to protect their nation's sovereignty. He was aware that it was not only necessary to provide the soldiers with rigorous physical training, but also to instill in them a sense of discipline in their thought processes. They were no longer considered insurgents, but rather troops serving a democratic Venezuela and defenders of the country's hard-won democracy.

The acts taken by Alejandro were not overlooked by those fighting for the opposition. There was an upsurge in the number of reports detailing attempted reconnaissance and cyberattacks on their military networks. It was quite evident that the opposition, which received support from Cuba and Russia, was stepping up their activities. Alejandro maintained his composure under the intense strain, remaining confidence in the resiliency of their recently trained warriors as well as the unyielding spirit of their people.

The importance of Sofia as the leader and voice of their revolt rose. She used her journalism to mobilize her fellow Venezuelans and hold their new leadership accountable, using her pen like a weapon and utilizing it as a weapon against the new regime. Her writings highlighted any instances of corruption, guaranteeing that their recently established democracy would not experience the same failures as their former authoritarian administration did.

On the other hand, the sound of her voice made her an easy target. The threats became increasingly overt while the warnings were only faintly concealed under the remarks of her detractors. She refused to be silenced despite the risks because she believed that her responsibility to her nation was much more important than her own personal safety.

The freshly independent Venezuela is now confronted with the unforgiving reality of their newfound autonomy. They are in a difficult position because they are stuck between the expectations they have for their bright future and the impending danger of a new battle. Alejandro and Sofia have taken a bold stance at the head of their nation's movement, guiding their people toward the promise of their hard-won independence.

Venezuela's newfound wealth, which was brought about by the assistance of the United States and international markets, was undoubtedly a welcome change of pace for the country, but it was not without its drawbacks. The fast development of the economy gave rise to the emergence of a new elite class of businesspeople who began to hold unprecedented levels of wealth and power.

Because of the fast entrance of foreign firms, there was a considerable need for local partners, which opened the door for a limited number of people to quickly gain fortune. They were able to demand conditions that suited them disproportionately and hence became the gatekeepers of the foreign direct investments that were streaming into the nation. The widening gap between rich and poor started to fuel dissatisfaction among the general populace.

Sofia, who keeps her ear to the ground, was the first person to catch up on this growing disquiet. Her essays began drawing attention to the growing economic gap and questioned whether the newly discovered democracy was only replacing one repressive dictatorship with another, although in a different guise. She believed that the answer lay in the latter. Her sharp journalism shifted its focus to the rich elite, bringing public attention to the exploitative behaviors of those individuals while also galvanizing opposition to those behaviors among the general populace.

Concurrently, the remnants of Maduro's administration, which are now reorganizing themselves under the flag of the opposition, took advantage of this chance. They started to agitate the situation even more by employing propaganda to bring attention to the income gap. The opposition took advantage of the circumstances by making empty promises to 'level the playing field' and' return the riches to the people.' They had discovered their rallying cry, and disgruntled Venezuelans, who felt they were being excluded from the economic miracle, began to listen.

On the other side, Alejandro found himself in a position that presented a number of difficulties. The newly created elites had become significant financial supporters of the defense budget, and the armed forces desperately required the funds that they provided. Nevertheless, he was also aware of the peril posed by a growing plutocracy. He was split between the urgent requirements of the nation's defense and the continued security of the country over the long term.

In the meantime, those opposed to us were keeping busy. They started acting more brazenly as Cuba and Russia began to back them up. The country went into a state of high alert as a result of an increase in the number of incidents involving sabotage and killings of important officials in the administration and the military.

The endurance of Venezuela's people, as well as the tenacity of their newly won independence, was being put to the test as the shadows of a previous nightmare began to reappear in the country. Alejandro and Sofia were forced to negotiate this perilous landscape in order to safeguard the ideas for which they had battled so hard. They were up against an old adversary who was operating under new conditions.

As Sofia continued her journalistic research on the growing privileged class, she became aware of a disturbing pattern. A significant number of the new elites had ties to the previous government, and some of them were even active in the opposition, using their wealth to covertly support the latter's operations. It seemed that the past was making its way back into the present, but it was obscured by the dazzling facade of economic growth. She decided to bring the truth to light, and published a groundbreaking revelation that sent the whole country into turmoil.

After Sofia made her discovery, Alejandro struggled to make sense of the implications. Some officers in the higher ranks of the military showed signs of divided loyalties as their hands were greased by members of the emerging privileged class. As Alejandro realized the implications of what he had learned, he felt a cold terror settle in his heart. Perhaps there were traitors in his own ranks. A purge was necessary, but it had to be done carefully to prevent the situation from becoming even more unstable.

The more Alejandro and Sofia looked into the matter, the more they also became aware of the growing foreign influence. Russia and Cuba were supporting the opposition with finances, weapons, and tactical help to reestablish control over Venezuela. This was done by using the opposition as proxies. The Cold War was a frightening reminder of the games that world powers play at the expense of smaller states, and seemed to have echoes of their times.

In the midst of this, the rebel group that had previously overthrown the dictatorship began to transform itself and adapt to the new obstacles it faced. The fall of Maduro didn't mean the end of their struggle for freedom, but only the beginning of a new phase in that struggle. The organization transformed from a guerrilla force to a more structured resistance movement and began recruiting new members and holding training sessions.

Despite the ever-increasing difficulties, there was a continuing spirit of optimism. The Venezuelan people had acquired a taste for freedom and weren't about to give it up so quickly when it was offered to them. The tenacity of the Venezuelan people is evident in the fact that they began to stage demonstrations throughout the country against the opposition and the elites. The people prepared to defend their country once again, under the leadership of Alejandro, who was guided by the unyielding voice of Sofia.

The groundwork had been laid for a different kind of struggle that would test the resilience of Venezuela's nascent democracy. This was no longer a simple uprising against an oppressive dictatorship, but a complicated ballet of politics, economics and power. And with each passing day, the echoes of the destroyed Eden became more and more audible.

The uprising had developed into a well-established movement by this point, and it served as the backbone of the country's defense against the resurgent forces that sought to smother its newly won independence. In spite of the growing night, Alejandro, ever the stoic commander, kept his composure and stood tall. He rallied his men and gave an inspiring address to the assembled throng, reminding them of the hardship they had been through and the future they were working to establish for themselves. His conviction shone like a lighthouse among the throngs of people who had gathered to hear him speak.

"Freedom is not something that happens; rather, it is a process." We have gotten this procedure under way, and we will see it through to its conclusion. Every single one of us is a defender of Venezuela, and we have an obligation to protect not just our country but also our rights and our future. Keep your head up and your shoulders back. Together, we are Venezuela!"

During this time, Sofia worked relentlessly, her articles presenting a vivid picture of the harsh reality of the socio-economic scene.

Every word that she put on paper was a defiance to the people in power, a call to arms for the common people, and a guiding light to the truth in the midst of confusion. Her writing became her sword, cutting through falsehoods and propaganda to expose the real nature of the opposition and their foreign masters. She used her pen as a sword to unveil the actual face of the opposition.

The risks associated with their combined efforts were significant. Both Alejandro and Sofia found themselves in the sights of the adversary, and the fate of their lives hung in the balance as a result. But despite this, they did not give up; instead, the challenges they faced made them more determined.

A portentous symbol appeared as the story came to an end. The data gathered by the rebels revealed that they had deciphered a message that suggested the opposition was planning a huge onslaught. On the horizon, there was a storm that was forming, and it threatened to envelop Venezuela in strife all over again.

From the headquarters of the insurgent group, Alejandro kept his gaze unwavering and unmoved as he surveyed the skyline of the city, which was in the path of the approaching storm. In the dark of the night, Sofia came up to him and put her hand on his shoulder.

Her voice was barely audible above the howling wind as she spoke to Alejandro. "The echoes of the lost Eden grow louder, Alejandro," she murmured. "But so does the roar of the phoenix." We are not going to give in to the darkness this time."

They remained huddled together as the first droplets of rain began to fall, signaling the beginning of the storm, and were prepared to face whatever came after it. It's possible that the echoes of the lost Eden are still being heard, but so are the screams of the phoenix, who is eager to rise again from the ashes of the challenges it has faced.

The story of their struggle had not yet reached its conclusion, but the message was crystal clear: Venezuela would fight no matter what. Its spirit, which was represented by the firm forms of Alejandro and

Sofia, was unbroken and would not bend down to the darkness that was drawing closer.

This was the calm before the storm, and it was a monument to the resiliency of the team in the face of overwhelming odds. Even though the echoes of the Eden that had been lost would continue to resonate, the Phoenix was truly prepared to rise, to guard, and if necessary, to reclaim the Eden that it so dearly loved.

Our narrative comes to an end with that idea, and we are left with a setting that is fraught with suspense, anxiety, and the irrepressible spirit of a nation that is on the verge of collapse.

EPILOGUE: "THE HORIZON BEYOND"

The headquarters of the rebels are now the nerve core of the new Venezuela, which is emerging from the ashes of its own stormy past. Alejandro, who was now considered a national hero, was extremely busy directing the defenses and getting ready for the storm that was looming in the distance. On the other side, Sofia had gone from being a solitary voice crying out in the desert to being the guiding light of truth for a nation that yearned for openness and justice.

Even though their voyage had been arduous and riddled with difficulties, a glimmer of optimism had been preserved throughout the ordeal. The flickering torch of revolt was kept alive thanks to the leadership and military expertise of Alejandro, as well as Sofia's zealousness in her journalistic pursuits. They had a long way to go before the battle was ended, but they were ready to confront it together.

The atmosphere in the streets of Caracas was positively electrifying. People from every imaginable background came together in support of their cause. The public's resistance to the Maduro opposition was fueled by the revelations of corruption and authoritarianism that Sofia brought to light. Inequality was no longer tolerated as the standard; rather, it was recognized for what it actually was: a cancerous growth that ate away at the social fabric of their society.

Even though Cuba and Russia supported the opposition, the government of the United States offered Sofia and Alejandro the assistance they desperately required. The fact that the rebels received assistance in the form of weapons, funding, and advisors provoked more discussions regarding the role of foreign powers, but it did not diminish the effectiveness of the rebels' defense.

But despite the hectic preparations and the mounting pressure, Sofia and Alejandro still managed to find peaceful solace in each other's company throughout the day. Their connection had grown stronger as a result of the challenges they had faced together and their shared aspirations for the future of their nation. The love that had been kindled in the midst of the uprising now protected them from the growing chill of the approaching storm.

As the days went by, it appeared as though the echoes of the lost Eden were stronger, while at the same time, the foreboding rumble of the impending storm became louder. In spite of this, the Venezuelan people maintained their resolve, and the stubborn figures of Sofia and Alejandro, who continued their arduous attempts to protect their treasured land, served as a symbol of the resilience of the Venezuelan people.

The future was cloudy, and there was a myriad of obstacles to overcome. However, even as they were on the verge of yet another conflict, the hope of a fresh start encouraged them to continue fighting. The long night filled with desolation had finally come to an end, making room for the dawning of hope. The Phoenix had risen, and despite the fact that the darkness was gathering once more, they knew deep down in their hearts that they would battle the shadows and come out on top.

Because Venezuela was their Garden of Eden and their homeland. And they would battle to defend it, no matter what the cost may be. Because the echoes of the lost Eden served not just as memories of the past but also as a clarion call to construct a better future for all of humanity. No matter how severe the storm, the resilient spirit of Venezuela, like that of the Phoenix, will continue to soar above it.

As a result, the trip proceeded in the direction of the horizon beyond, into a future in which freedom would rule and aspirations would flourish. A future that was worth fighting for according to them.

The seeds of revolt had been planted in these courageous hearts, and they had grown into a huge tree that now casts its protecting shadow over the region that they loved. This would be their legacy, a monument to the resiliency they possessed. It was their version of Venezuela. And the echo of their voyage would ring throughout the years, a timeless narrative of defiance, tenacity, and redemption.

ABOUT THE AUTHOR

Robert Dobbs is an accomplished author, US Army Airborne veteran, and dedicated public servant with a rich background in international relations, management consulting, and education. His life experiences and academic achievements have informed his writing, which focuses on themes of resilience, leadership, and the power of personal growth.

Born and raised in Wisconsin in the United States, Robert's military career began when he enlisted in the US Army Airborne. During his service, he was deployed to several overseas locations, where he developed a strong sense of discipline and camaraderie. After completing his military duties, he transitioned into civilian life, eager to continue serving his community in other ways.

With a passion for public service, Robert spent a decade in local elected office, where he tackled various issues related to governance, social welfare, and economic development. At the same time, he was appointed to serve on a board for the Supreme Court of Wisconsin, further showcasing his dedication to the betterment of society.

Robert's keen interest in international affairs led him to spend ten years working in the Middle East and Central Asia as an education and management consultant. Here, he played an essential role in fostering understanding and cooperation between diverse cultures and organizations.

With a Master's degree in International Relations, an MBA, and a Bachelor of Science in Public Administration, Robert's education has provided him with a solid foundation for his work in both the public and private sectors. His unique combination of military, political, and international experience has given him a distinctive voice as an author, offering readers a fresh perspective on global issues and the human experience.

In his personal life, Robert is a devoted husband and father.